Informal Reckonings

From court-based diversion programmes to the South African Truth and Reconciliation Commission, so-called 'informal justice' practices have, since the 1970s, enjoyed great popularity. This 'reparative turn' provides reasons for both hope and concern. While conflict resolution techniques, such as civil mediation, restorative justice and reparations, provide opportunities for greater citizen participation in justice, they also raise the spectre of expanded state and social control. *Informal Reckonings* seeks to elucidate the prospects and perils of 'informal justice' by situating those practices within the 'informal–formal justice complex'—a sociocultural formation within which reputedly antinomic formal and informal legal tendencies combine to reproduce the juridical status quo. In order to chart a course out of the limiting space of this 'complex', this book proposes that mediation, restorative justice and reparations take on the features of informal 'counterpublics' that, as arenas for the expression and mobilisation of social and legal criticism, create momentum toward a truly transformative justice.

Andrew Woolford is Associate Professor of Sociology at the University of Manitoba. He is author of *Between Justice and Certainty: Treaty Making in British Columbia* (2005, UBC Press) and has published articles on Canadian aboriginal peoples, genocide and conflict resolution in journals such as the *Law and Society Review, Critical Criminology, Canadian Journal of Sociology, Journal of Human Rights* and *Social Justice*.

R.S. Ratner is Professor Emeritus (Sociology) at the University of British Columbia. He is co-editor of *State Control: Criminal Justice Politics in Canada* (1987, UBC Press) and *Challenges and Perils: Social Democracy in Neoliberal Times* (2005, Fernwood Books). His research interests are in the fields of social movements, critical criminology and political sociology. His current research project is a cross-cultural study of genocide reparations.

Informal Reckonings

Conflict resolution in mediation, restorative justice and reparations

Andrew Woolford and R.S. Ratner

Routledge·Cavendish
Taylor & Francis Group
a GlassHouse book

First edition published 2008 by Routledge-Cavendish
2 Park Square, Milton Park, Abingdon, Oxon OX14 4RN

Simultaneously published in the USA and Canada
by Routledge-Cavendish
270 Madison Ave, New York, NY 10016

A GlassHouse book

Routledge-Cavendish is an imprint of the Taylor & Francis Group,
an informa business

© 2008 Andrew Woolford and R.S. Ratner

Typeset in Times by
RefineCatch Limited, Bungay, Suffolk
Printed and bound in Great Britain by
Biddles Ltd., King's Lynn, Norfolk

British Library Cataloguing in Publication Data
A catalogue record for this book is available from the British Library

Library of Congress Cataloging-in-Publication Data
Woolford, Andrew John, 1971–
    Informal reckonings : conflict resolution in mediation, restorative
justice, and reparations / Andrew Woolford and R.S. Ratner. —
1st ed.
        p. cm.
    Includes bibliographical references.
    ISBN-13: 978–1–904385–86–8 (pbk)
    ISBN-10: 1–904385–86–9 (pbk)
    ISBN-13: 978–0–415–42934–4 (hbk)
    ISBN-10: 0–415–42934–X (hbk)
    [etc.]
    1. Reparation (criminal justice). 2. Mediation. 3. Restorative justice.
4. Dispute resolution (Law) 5. Restitution. 6. Criminal justice,
Administration of. 7. Truth commissions. I. Ratner, Robert, 1938–
II. Title.
    K970.W66 2008
    347'.09—dc22

                                      2007027731

ISBN10: 1–904385–86–9 (pbk)
ISBN13: 978–1–904385–86–8 (pbk)

ISBN10: 0–415–42934–X (hbk)
ISBN13: 978–0–415–42934–4 (hbk)

eISBN10: 0–203–93873–9
eISBN13: 978–0–203–93873–7

Contents

Preface

For some, 'informal' methods of conflict resolution—for example, mediation, restorative justice, reparations—offer hope for overcoming the alienating and over-professionalised conditions of 'formal' law. By stepping outside the restrictive space of law and encouraging people to solve their own problems, these proponents of 'informal justice' argue, we might be able to achieve resolutions that satisfy all parties and help to repair our damaged societies. But for others, informal conflict resolution represents a false hope. These critics claim that, rather than empowering individuals and communities, informal conflict resolution practices simply allow the state to broaden its reach by enlisting the services of ancillary professionals who actually widen the net of social control. In this sense, informal justice is perceived to be little more than formal justice by other means.

This debate has carried on for some time and has reached a point at which a new set of scholars has begun to question its very terms: are there really distinct spaces of justice—the formal and the informal? Does social control emanate solely from the state? Or does control also function at a distance from such centres of calculation? Building on this literature, we argue that informal and formal modes of conflict resolution are entwined in an 'informal–formal justice complex'—a sociocultural formation through which these supposed antinomic tendencies combine to reproduce the juridical status quo. Based on this analysis, we raise critical concerns about the 'reparative turn' that has brought mediation, restorative justice and reparations to greater prominence in contemporary times, and which too often serves to bolster, rather than to assail, neoliberal and juridical domination. But rather than dismiss these supposed 'informal' conflict resolution practices out of hand, we suggest that they possess a communicative potential that might be harnessed to the projects of social and juridical transformation. In order that they might fulfil this role, we propose that these forms of conflict resolution take on the strategic sensibilities of 'informal counterpublics': that is, they must be deliberative spaces designed to disrupt the legal status quo and to open up new justice possibilities.

This book would not have been possible without the help of many sources and individuals. The two authors began work on this topic under the auspices of the Program on Dispute Resolution at the University of British Columbia, a Community University Research Alliance (CURA) project funded by the Social Sciences and Humanities Research Council (SSHRC). We would like to thank John Hogarth and Sharon Sutherland for their ongoing support throughout our involvement in this project. The mediators and restorative justice practitioners whom we interviewed in the course of this research, and who provided feedback on related papers, were also of great help. In addition, the support of a SSHRC Standard Research Grant enabled us to carry out investigations into reparations politics. The research assistance of Murray Shaw, Rosa Sevy and Stefan Wolejszo has been invaluable to this latter project.

We have also benefited from conversations with, and input from, various colleagues, including George Pavlich and Bryan Hogeveen. Finally, and by way of reparation, we dedicate this book to Gloria, Jess, Ella and Robyn.

Andrew Woolford and R.S. Ratner
June 2007

Chapter 1

Formal and informal justice

The topography of law: the formal and the informal

Law is often discussed as though it is a physical space. It has been described metaphorically as an 'arena' or a 'field' (Gilson and Mnookin, 1994; Harnett, 1985; Mason, 1999). But if law is a field, what are its contours? Does it have an inside and an outside? Are some practices more central to this field (the 'formal'), while others are more marginal and secondary (the 'informal')? In modern, Western, capitalist societies, the answer to this question is often taken to be self-evident. We commonly refer to state-administered and bureaucratic justice processes as 'formal', while negotiated and meditated justice processes are designated as 'informal'. Simply put, 'informal justice' refers to those forms of justice that are said to take place outside of the formal court-room, in settings that are less rule-bound and adversarial. For many critics of 'formal justice', informal practices hold the promise of a justice that is more empowering, participatory and accessible, while, at the same time, less alienating, costly and adversarial (Bush and Folger, 1994).

Over the past few decades, we have seen new dispute resolution practices rising to the fore, claiming the status of 'informal' justice and claiming to 'do law differently'. The three forms of so-called informal justice that we discuss in this book—mediation, restorative justice and reparations—exemplify this trend. By 'mediation', we mean specifically practices of civil dispute resolution in which a 'neutral' intermediary assists conflicting parties in arriving at a consensual resolution, sparing them the time, cost and combativeness of the courtroom.[1] The mediator is not asked to decide the case for the parties; rather, using a variety of negotiation and communication techniques, the mediator helps to 'facilitate' a discussion that is directed toward reaching an agreed-upon solution.

'Restorative justice' follows similar principles, but focuses largely on 'criminal' conflicts. Restorative justice meetings bring together victims and

---

1 Some would question the assumption of mediator 'neutrality' (see, e.g., Cobb and Rifkin, 1991; Rifkin et al, 1991) and the goals of time/cost savings.

offenders—and, in some cases, their friends, families and fellow community members—in facilitated meetings to discuss the consequences of, and potential resolutions for, criminal acts. Like mediation, restorative justice is intended to be a participatory and empowering form of justice, which removes judicial agency from the grip of legal professionals and places it largely in the hands of citizens. In restorative justice encounters, victims and offenders are invited to recount their versions of the events that transpired. In addition, the offender often receives a chance to explain the motivation behind the misdeed, while the victim usually gets an opportunity to impress upon the offender the suffering that has been caused. Throughout the process, family, friends and community members may be able to offer input in the form of comments on the character of the victim and offender, as well as the wider consequences of the criminal act and by suggesting how the offence may be remedied.

Finally, 'reparations', as we use the term, features a variety of responses to past injustices, including tribunals, truth commissions, commemoration, restitution, lustration,[2] and symbolic and material compensation. Our focus is less on the formal zones of this field, within which international courts—such as the International Criminal Tribunals for the former Yugoslavia and Rwanda—have been established; we are more concerned with those mechanisms that seek to attend to collective wrongs and collective suffering without recourse to courts and trials. For example, although truth commissions are, in some cases, affiliated with or loosely connected to legal or quasi-legal proceedings (as is the case in Sierra Leone), they establish public hearings and truth-telling ceremonies designed to reveal previously unacknowledged or actively denied political crimes and human rights violations. Likewise, commemorative projects—such as the establishment of memorial museums or days—and compensatory programs—which may involve the dispersal of symbolic gestures (e.g. apologies) and/or material goods (e.g. monetary payments) to wronged groups—serve to publicly recognise previous injustices and symbolise an end to conflictive group relations. In most cases, all of these efforts represent attempts to prevent past conflicts from stagnating in the courts, within which excessive time and resources would be required to bring about their resolution.

Based on these brief descriptions of mediation, restorative justice and reparations, we can begin to identify some of the 'informal' characteristics that unite these justice practices:

- they are intended to facilitate the participation and empowerment of the parties involved in the conflict without necessary recourse to legal professionals;

2 'Lustration' refers to the practice of removing from power those civil servants who were complicit with a previous authoritarian regime.

- they are adaptable to the specific conditions of the conflict at hand, rather than rigidly bound by rules;
- their legitimacy does not derive from state authorisation, but rather from the representative and deliberative involvement of concerned parties, as well as participant satisfaction.

Supporters of these 'alternative' forms of conflict resolution contend that, in contrast, the formal justice system fails on these three grounds. The court-based system of formal justice disempowers the parties to a dispute by making legal professionals the key participants in the dispute resolution process. It also applies rigid rules of formal law that inhibit creative solutions to societal conflicts and problems. Finally, formal law serves the primary function of reinforcing state legitimacy rather than restoring positive community relations (cf. Christie, 1977; Van Ness and Heetderks Strong, 1997).

It must be acknowledged, however, that these so-called informal modes of 'dispute' or 'conflict' resolution often receive resources and endorsement from the reputed bastion of formalism: the state. Mediation techniques have been used as a means for clearing the clutter and backlog of the civil courtroom, and for reducing the costs of justice; restorative justice has been broadly accepted as a tool for dealing with youth and those committing 'less serious' crimes; reparative bodies, such as the South African Truth and Reconciliation Commission, have been implemented by states in places where formal justice appears too difficult to achieve. This raises the question: do these practices represent a transformation of the legal field? Or are they simply part of a reconstituted, yet still persistent, legal order? Our task in this book is not only to situate these 'informal' practices in relation to the field of law, but also to understand them in their broader social and historical contexts. Why have these practices emerged en masse at the present socio-historical moment? Moreover, do they carry potential to serve as catalysts for progressive social change?

Up to this point, we have placed the words 'informal' and 'formal' within quotation marks to highlight that these are problematic terms, which are contested on several grounds. For example, questions have been raised as to whether or not these terms truly designate separate realms of legal activity (Fitzpatrick, 1995). What we refer to as the 'formal' system of law—e.g. the codified law and its application in courtroom settings—has always contained 'informal' elements. This point was driven home for one of this book's authors when he was called to court as witness for the Crown in a case involving the uttering of threats and assault with a weapon. Ten months earlier, on a leisurely camping outing, he had asked a neighbouring camper to turn down the volume on his stereo, to which the neighbour had responded by taking a crossbow from his tent and threatening to kill the co-author. Once in the formal courtroom, however, before facing the judge, the co-author was informed by the Crown attorney that a plea bargain was in process. The

Crown was considering a suspended sentence with probationary conditions, based upon the defendant's participation in Alcoholics Anonymous and anger management programmes during the time following the incident. With the blessing of the co-author, the plea bargain was accepted and the case was informally negotiated to resolution, literally on the steps of the courthouse.

In addition, it has also been suggested that, when studied closely, 'informal' practices, such as mediation, often reveal formal patterns of action and outcome (Pavlich, 1996a) and operate to reproduce, rather than to challenge, the hegemony of law (Pavlich, 2005; Woolford and Ratner, 2007). For example, informal justice programmes tend to siphon off cases that might otherwise overburden the formal justice system and thereby, through this 'clutter-clearing' function, serve to bolster, rather than to counter, formal justice. If, however, the formal law is as its informal critics describe it—an adversarial practice that privileges the roles of professionals, while excluding wider citizen participation—then this complicity in reproducing legal domination clearly detracts from claims that informal justice represents an 'alternative' to formal justice. Moreover, the close relationship between informal and formal justice raises questions about the degree to which informal justice presents an oppositional challenge to formal justice.

We take as our starting point not the assumption that there exist mutually exclusive formal and informal aspects of law, but instead the notion that the complexity of law is poorly reflected in the formal–informal dichotomy. It may seem, then, that the language of the informal and the formal is unhelpful, and that it should be discarded; we will instead elaborate the idea of an 'informal–formal justice complex' to describe a cultural and political formation in which adversarial/punitive and conciliatory/restorative justice forms coexist and overlap in relative harmony, despite their apparent contradictions. This idea allows us to acknowledge that there are informal and formal elements of law, even if there are not fully formal or informal systems. It also allows us to approach the question of whether or not these informal elements or 'moments' hold any potential as a space from which can be launched an internal critique that challenges the ways in which current legal practices tend to reflect the interests of dominant social actors and exclude significant public input.

The informal–formal justice complex will receive greater attention in the next chapter; for now, it will suffice to say that we intend to problematise the informal–formal binary so that we can better understand the space in which new justice processes emerge, as well as their potential to counter hegemonic patterns of law and domination.

Informal justice?

Informal justice, in the forms noted above and in others, is argued to have had a long history. Its earliest manifestations are often located in small-scale, kinship-based societies of the distant past (Zehr, 1990; Weitekamp, 2003). In these 'acephalous' (or headless) societies (Michalowski, 1985), egalitarian relations were complemented by conflict resolution mechanisms directed toward righting wrongs and re-establishing community harmony. While blood revenge, retribution and ritual punishments were not uncommon as means for correcting deviance, restitution was the method most widely used in these societies (Weitekamp, 2003).

Informal justice is also considered to have been the paradigmatic justice strategy for various indigenous peoples. While, as Laroque (1997) notes, the anthropological record is often portrayed in an overly simplistic fashion that ignores the punitive forms of conflict resolution employed by some indigenous communities, several indigenous groups did utilise (and continue to utilise) conciliatory justice practices. The Maori of New Zealand, for example, use what is called 'Marae' justice, which they have continued to practise even after colonisation and the attempted imposition of Pakeha (non-Maori) justice. For most minor cases, and even for more serious conflicts involving sexual or child abuse, the families of disputing parties gather to talk things through, to get to the root of the problem and to create a plan to deal with the matter. Rarely are such cases reported to the formal authorities. Moreover, Marae justice has now received formal recognition in the form of the Children, Young Persons and Their Families Act (1989), which mandates the use of Maori family group conferencing methods for youth offences before they are brought to family court (Consedine, 2003).

Several examples of informal justice can also be noted among the early colonial settlers of North America. Indeed, as Auerbach (1983) illustrates, Puritan and Quaker communities in colonial America exhibited a strong scepticism toward law and state involvement in everyday life, and held informal negotiation between disputants to be more consistent with Christian approaches to justice. When conflict arose in these communities, it was considered an antisocial act to take one's fellow community member to a court of law; instead, matters were resolved by a local notable, who was familiar with both of the parties to the conflict and held moral authority vested through his or her community status.

In Western societies, informal justice is commonly thought to have disappeared or receded after the state 'stole crime' (Christie, 1977) and conflict from communities. Even after the beginning of state centralisation and formal legal power in roughly the twelfth century, however, informal justice has had a continued presence in these societies, even if only in the 'shadow' of the formal law (Mnookin and Kornhauser, 1979; Harrington, 1985). Evidence of the persistence of so-called informal justice can be identified in figures such as the West German Schiedsman (a local conflict conciliator available for the voluntary resolution of disputes) and the French juge de paix (a system of locally elected justice officials established after the French Revolution, and designed to increase access to justice and mediate disputes within the communes). Nonetheless, over time, informal justice practices have become marginalised and secondary to state-driven processes of conflict resolution.

The marginalisation of informal conflict resolution practices began with the movement towards state consolidation, whereby rulers sought greater control over, and definition of, their populations and national boundaries. The impetus behind this consolidation came, in part, from the needs of an emerging industrial system that required workforce regulation, as well as controls over those who rejected work. In Britain, those forced off the land through the process of enclosures were 'freed' from serfdom to choose work within the factories that were multiplying across the country; many opted not to work rather than to subject themselves to gruelling labour for long hours in terrible conditions for inadequate pay. Legal controls were thus a means by which these individuals could, for instance, be branded 'vagrants' and forced into work camps or imprisoned. We must, however, be careful not to reduce the emergence of legal hegemony to a mechanistic function of changing economic conditions, because culture also played a role. A cultural shift toward more individual, competitive and rights-based discourses was simultaneously occurring, leaving behind the community connections that made informal justice practices more readily operational (Auerbach, 1983). As urban density increased, and as individuals with different belief and value systems began to live among one another, conflict was no longer simply a matter of neighbours working things out; instead, it often involved people, who were unfamiliar with one another, seeking to advance their own individual interests.

But the inverse relationship between capital and informal justice is not as straightforward as it may appear, and capitalists, while calling for greater formalisation in some sectors (e.g. crime control and property rights), also saw the utility of informal justice for their own practices. Thus, while changing economic relations destroyed the grounds on which informal justice systems were built, some informal justice practices nonetheless continued. Indeed, informal justice was the justice of choice in many commercial interactions. From the early days of the capitalist system, merchants and traders viewed the formal justice system as an inefficient and expensive means of conflict resolution. They preferred to work out conflicts in accordance with the informal customs of business, rather than the law of the courts (Auerbach, 1983; Dezalay, 1994; Heydebrand, 2003) and, in this manner, the capitalist class played a crucial role in the persistence of informal justice. But this group also contributed to the further entanglement of formal and informal justices. For the business-minded, informal justice was not simply a means for resolving conflict in a manner appropriate to commercial norms and standards: it was, more importantly, an economically rational justice option, because it was much more cost effective than lengthy court battles. Given that their use of informal justice was primarily instrumental, merchants and businesspersons were not averse to using the formal justice system when they felt that the case was serious enough to merit court attention, or when they felt that an adversary could be intimidated by the prospects of a lengthy legal dispute. In this manner, their embrace of informal justice did not represent a disavowal of formal justice; indeed, it contributed to the increased valuation of formal justice, because the courts were reserved for more contentious cases (Dezalay, 1994).

The hegemony of formal justice became more pronounced in the policies and practices of the welfare state that, following World War II, became a dominant paradigm for Western governments. The welfare state regulation regime functioned through a combination of Keynesian political rationalities and Fordist accumulation strategies (Tickell and Peck, 1995), which together entailed the heightening of state-steering activities in the economy and in society. In respect of justice (in addition to other areas of public service), we see, during this period, a growing role for state-based service providers, experts and professionals. While this cadre of actors was charged with seemingly valuable justice tasks—e.g. increasing the likelihood of offender rehabilitation, expanding citizen access to justice—they carried out their duties in ways that accelerated the penetration of governance into everyday life (Cohen, 1985). Under the auspices of this state formation, justice became more professionalised and dispensed 'from above'.

The initial decline of the welfare state in the 1960s, as well as heightened criticism of the state through the social movement activism of this period, created conditions amenable to a revival of legal informalism. In the 1970s, a general dissatisfaction arose in respect of the power of professionals and the state to control people's lives, and some envisioned a broad reclamation of social services from the state's grasp. Discourses of deprofessionalisation and deinstitutionalisation provided an ideational framework for imagining forms of justice that would allow for greater citizen involvement in, and control over, dispute resolution processes (see Illich, 1977; also Illich et al, 1977). The community, rather than the state, became the basis for a reconstructed justice.

Ironically, this ground-level activism was concordant with the subsequent rationality of an ascendant neoliberal ethos—most apparent in the Reagan and Thatcher economic policies of the 1980s—which strongly criticised the presuppositions of the welfare state on the grounds that it represented a cumbersome and inefficient network of regulatory controls that slowed the progress of globalising capital. Under these conditions, the practices of informal justice, although formed in a countercultural space concerned with opposing state and corporate domination, were now complemented by an emerging neoliberal political rationality that sought the reduction of state intervention for entirely different reasons. Indeed, informal justice found its practices at risk of co-optation and redirection under this new influence, because the ideologues of neoliberalism sought to transfer managerial responsibility to individuals and communities in order to weaken state control and loosen restraints on capital (Burchell, 1993; Rose, 1996).

Amidst these swirling political and economic developments, informal justice became a more active movement. According to Harrington and Merry
(1988), this movement was guided by three frames of reference:

- a pragmatic concern with the improved delivery of legal services, including access to justice;
- a hope that society could be transformed through the spread of informal
  justice, allowing communities to take ownership of their problems and
  the solutions to these problems;
- a drive toward individual empowerment that would allow people to
  improve their conflict resolution skills, so that they could apply these
  skills in multiple problematic situations.

There are clear overlaps between these three frames of reference, but also
signs of an emerging contradiction within the informal justice movement as it
sought to provide both an alternative and a complement to the formal justice
system (Pavlich, 2005). The first, or 'pragmatic', frame of reference suggests a
justice that is complementary and improves the 'delivery of justice', whereas
the second, or 'transformative/community', frame of reference suggests the
need for greater distance between the community and the formal justice system, and thus speaks of a distinct alternative to the latter. The third option,
the imparting of improved individual conflict resolution skills, resonates with
neoliberal discourses of citizen responsibility and empowerment. Thus, the
informal justice movement is divided across these axes, making it difficult to
sustain a universal notion of justice (Pavlich, 1996a). While social movements
usually represent, to some extent, a negotiated achievement between competing frames and visions of the movement's goals and meanings (Diani, 1992),
the splitting of the informal justice movement between oppositional and
complementary stances, in relation to the state and the status quo, resulted in
schisms within the informal justice movement that would prove difficult to
bridge.

The movement has also developed in distinct ways in different areas of law.
For this reason, we focus on informal justice techniques as they have been
applied in three different sites: mediation in civil law; restorative justice in
criminal law; reparations in domestic and international law. Within each of
these sites, we see a diversity of 'alternative' justice practices emerging, each
varying in terms of the degree to which they:

- co-operate with the formal justice system;
- espouse either social justice or managerialist goals;
- resist or embrace professionalisation.

Mediation, for example, has developed significantly from its early status as a
community-based and culturally embedded dispute resolution technique into

a complex assemblage of legal and quasi-legal practices. As we shall see in Chapter 3, in the 1970s, the 'community mediation' movement sought to re-establish the community as a locus for informal justice, combining communitarianism with themes of social justice that were emergent in this period of heightened political activism. By situating dispute resolution in the community and in the hands of lay activists, it was hoped that the community capacity for autonomy would increase, and that the conditions would be laid for building community harmony and individual skills of peaceful conflict resolution. This movement, however, was the most informal, social justice-oriented and deprofessionalised of the mediation variants operating in the civil realm. Alongside community mediation, other mediation techniques found their way into small claims courts, human rights disputes and business disputes. Thus, for instance, in some jurisdictions, two neighbours in a dispute involving damage caused to the house of one by a fallen branch from an uncared-for tree in the yard of the other may find that they are mandated by the court to attend a 30-minute mediation session before their case is heard by a small claims court. Similarly, a professor accused of harassing a student with insulting and insensitive remarks may be asked by the university ombudsman to enter into mediation with the student, so that he might better understand the harm he has caused the student and have an opportunity to apologise. Finally, architects, contractors, builders, engineers and 'condo' owners may all find themselves in a mediated negotiation to establish who is going to pay the costs for sloppily erected buildings that are prone to leaks, mould and mildew soon after purchase. These latter cases tend to follow more formalised procedures (such as the time limits and evaluative techniques used by small claims mediators), to be more managerialist in their goals (such as in the ombudsman's goal to make peace and avoid bad publicity for the university) and to involve professionals in key roles (such as the lawyers who often represent the parties in construction disputes). In this manner, mediation has become a technique of formal law as much as it is an alternative to formal law.

Restorative justice is also becoming increasingly complex in respect of these three characteristics. In Chapter 4, we will detail how restorative justice emerged out of the social justice beliefs of faith communities (Mennonite and Quaker, most prominently), anti-prison activists and a variety of other criminal justice reformers (see also Van Ness and Heetderks Strong, 1997). From the earliest moments of its conceptualisation, it was described as a values-based approach and as a progressive alternative to the formal criminal justice system. This latter 'system' was criticised for its retributive qualities, which, rather than heal and rehabilitate offenders, were said to reinforce offender commitment to crime by shaming them in such a stigmatising manner that their reintegration back into society became near impossible (Braithwaite, 1989). In contrast, restorative justice, through methods such as victim–offender mediations, healing circles and family group conferences, sought to re-establish community connections for offenders through facilitated face-to-face interactions involving victims, family members and, in some cases, representatives from the broader community. Through these volunteer-led meetings, an opportunity was provided for offender, victim and community to come to an agreement about the crime and how to deal with its aftermath.

But restorative justice, like mediation, found different applications in different settings. In some communities, restorative justice programmes are operated largely on a voluntary basis and seek community referrals as their primary source for cases; it is more often the case that restorative justice programmes must co-operate with state agencies in order to maintain their operations. Government funding is required to rent office space and to pay for administrative costs. Referrals are obtained from judges, state or Crown attorneys and police officers. Professional and technical training is provided for paid staff to ensure that they are schooled in the latest restorative justice techniques. For example, in a not-atypical case, a restorative justice programme may begin work with an offender when she is referred to the programme by a state or Crown attorney, who has assessed that the offender has taken responsibility for her actions and is likely to benefit from diversionary treatment. This offender will then meet with a restorative justice case planner, who, in some cases through consultation with the victim, will assist the offender in drawing up an agreement that will serve as a sanction for her crime. This agreement is likely to involve some form of community service, as well as place limitations on the offender's behaviour (e.g. no alcohol and a 10 pm curfew). It will subsequently be presented to a judge for approval and for any additional sanctions that the judge may add, based on legal precedent. Thus, as in mediation, we see different degrees of reliance on formal justice or state support, emphasis on social justice values, and practitioner professionalisation among restorative justice programmes.

Finally, the field of reparations politics offers examples ranging from the largely informal—spontaneous or planned commemorations that are entirely citizen-led—to quasi-formal—state-established truth commissions that carry the authority to make recommendations to the state in respect of how an unsavoury past should be handled (see Hayner, 2002). Victim-based reparations are a relatively recent development: historically speaking, reparations were a negotiated settlement between formerly warring states through which the defeated nation would agree to pay compensation to the victor. In the aftermath of World War II and, more specifically, the Nazi-perpetrated Holocaust, however, Jewish groups mobilised to demand compensation for Jewish material losses and physical suffering. This eventually resulted in an agreement between these groups, the state of Israel and West Germany for individual and collective indemnification for German crimes against the Jewish people (Sagi, 1980). This is an example of an informally negotiated settlement and, combined with the International Military Tribunal at Nuremberg, it provided an immediate response to Nazi crimes. In the 1970s, further efforts were made to deal with German war crimes. Young West Germans began to question their parents and grandparents about their roles in the war and in the destruction of European Jewry. Artistic and literary commemorations were designed to educate and to incite Germans to 'remember'. In addition, trials of Nazi perpetrators continued throughout the post-war era, providing frequent reminders of the terrible deeds committed in the name of National Socialism. These, among other activities, represented the combined force of informal and formal justice in dealing with the past that, in many ways, transformed West German society. Moreover, the West German post-war experience became a model for other nations seeking to address historical injustices. Yet not all of these nations possessed the resources of West Germany, particularly when it came to making large monetary payouts and prosecuting perpetrators. Nations such as South Africa, Argentina and El Salvador instead opted to establish truth commissions as a less formal means for learning from, and healing, historical injustices.

Returning to the three defining characteristics discussed above—the degree to which informal justice programmes co-operate with formal justice institutions, adopt social justice or managerialist goals and accept or reject professionalisation—it is clear that reparations programmes experience great difficulty in trying to adhere to any pure notion of informality. These programmes typically cannot avoid some form of co-operation with the formal justice system, because reparative responses, at minimum, typically require state legislative support to enforce, for example, compensatory payments or the establishment of days of remembrance. Furthermore, as these various reparative processes run their course, although they may begin with broad promises of social justice, they often finish seeking modest outcomes that are more readily attainable under current political conditions. In this regard, the South African Truth and Reconciliation Commission was unable to meet the broad healing and redistributive goals it had set for itself, settling instead for offering a public forum to provide recognition (and minimal repair) to victims of apartheid's gross human rights violations. Finally, although legal and state professionals do not necessarily occupy their formal roles when participating in informal reparative processes, they are still often called upon to serve as truth commissioners and negotiators.

A common feature of all of these 'informal' justice types (mediation, restorative justice and reparations) is that they are of relatively recent vintage. While traces of each practice can be located throughout history, it is within the last few decades—particularly since the 1970s—that they have become most prominent. This leads us to suggest that we have witnessed a 'reparative turn' during this period, a shift bolstered by social, political and economic developments occurring at a global level. In particular, as discussed in the last section, the ascendancy of political neoliberalism, combined with growing

economic and cultural globalisation, has contributed to an environment conducive to conciliatory politics. At the risk of oversimplifying, we attribute
some of the shift to emerging patterns of neoliberal political philosophy
that value the reduction of state infrastructure and the harnessing of local
energies toward improved governance. Such patterns include demands made
by an increasingly mobile capital for deregulation and flexibility so as to
enable a less restricted flow of global commerce. Informal justice is consistent with these patterns, because it offers a form of dispute resolution that
decreases state involvement, while potentially reinforcing state objectives
(e.g. maintaining social order). By providing justice options that are less regu-
lated and more fluid, informal justice coincidentally serves the needs of
capital.

This is not, however, to reduce informal justice to an ideological tool of the
ruling elite: informal justice is chosen and advocated by citizens not simply
because they are subordinates of an ascendant neoliberal hegemony, but
because such practices cohere with democratic and participatory sensibilities.
Simply put, informal justice, in its many forms, is a practice that ostensively
provides citizens with deliberative input into justice within their societies. Yet
it is a distinctly ambivalent practice, because it has the potential to further
desires for both increased social order and citizen empowerment. The question is: are these desires mutually exclusive? Or, perhaps more importantly,
can informal justice be separated from its order-maintenance function so
that its primary purpose is to enable citizen insights to take root and to
challenge dominant societal codes?

The corruption of informal justice

In the 1980s, critical socio-legal scholars and sociologists began to question
some of the more radical claims of informal justice. Those who saw informal
justice as a distinct alternative—as a non-bureaucratic, deprofessionalised,
community-oriented model of justice—were challenged, based on academic
evaluations of existing informal justice programmes (such as the community
justice centres in the USA: see Harrington, 1985). Rather than affording
communities a greater degree of autonomy, these programmes allegedly
increased the level of state and social control in society (see Abel, 1982;
Hofrichter, 1982; Tomasic, 1982). Since the beginning of the informal justice
movement, these critics argued, the reach of the state had been extended
and the net of social control cast wider. Stanley Cohen (1985), for example,
in his examination of community-based diversion programmes, suggests
that the disciplinary force of these programmes was applied to a broader
range of actors than ever before, in part because informal justice programmes
had provided the state with a cheaper and more efficient means to discipline those whose minor crimes might otherwise have been ignored by the
state.

In this sense, these 'state control' critics[3] of informal justice argued that informal justice is not an 'alternative' to formal justice; rather, it is a complement, and this complementarity has serious ramifications for community and individual autonomy because informal justice appears to bring state control directly into the lives of non-incarcerated citizens. In accordance with this logic, the more formal, pragmatic and professionalised elements of mediation, restorative justice and reparations would be expected to become dominant within informal justice, rendering it a tool of state domination. Moreover, through this state control lens, even those informal justice programmes claiming a social justice orientation would appear to be suspect. Community mediation centres would be viewed as indoctrinating citizens to become non-disputing subjects shorn of resistive tendencies. Restorative justice sessions, as well, would be seen as a means to pacify a 'criminal class' that is lashing out against a lack of social opportunity and status. Reparations processes would appear as a mere salve: an attempt to soothe restive populations still suffering the sting of past harms. Seeing all of these cases through a state control lens would reveal a directive state exploiting informal 'justice' to quell incipient political opposition.

State control theorists, however, would soon face their own challengers and detractors. In the later 1980s and early 1990s, a group of scholars influenced by the work of Michel Foucault, loosely referred to here as members of the school of 'governmentality studies', began to question the bipolar nature of the informalism–formalism and alternative–complement debates, suggesting that informal and formal practices overlap and mutually reinforce the field of juridical power. In the next chapter, we will contrast their work with that of Jürgen Habermas, whose theoretical corpus can be excavated to offer guidance for revitalised and reconstructed democratic practices of 'informal justice'. In this manner, we hope to reframe the problems and potentials of informal justice, and to articulate a clearer conceptualisation of the informal–formal justice complex.

Justice: the grand illusion?

Following the portrait we have painted of informal justice thus far, it would appear that justice is, if anything, illusory. As is often the case, the best intentions of justice reformers are rebuffed by an impervious system uninterested in fair-minded innovations. A resultant sense of impotency can suggest that there is no realisable means for improving the prospects for justice in the contemporary world.

3 Elsewhere in the literature, this group is referred to as 'social control' critics of informal justice (Pavlich, 1996b). In contrast, we opt for the phrase 'state control' critics because we wish to emphasise the degree to which these critics see social control as emanating directly from the state.

It would also appear that justice, as a unifying and universal concept, is increasingly problematic. Our confidence in the rightness of our liberal-democratic notion of justice has been shaken by increased awareness of other ways of doing justice. Anthropologists, philosophers and others have brought to our attention the fact that the presuppositions on which we base our notion of justice rest heavily on a Eurocentric normative framework that represents a failure to recognise other cultural configurations of the right and the good (Taylor, 1992). The law, which forms such a central part of our understandings of justice, is argued to be but one cultural expression of justice and one that is not always appropriate to other peoples, such as indigenous groups with their own distinct traditions of law. It might be that we will one day identify a common ethical core at the heart of all cultural models of justice, but, too often, attempts to find a universal basis for justice rest too heavily on one (dominant) cultural tradition. Moreover, attempts to comprehend alternative models of justice can be argued to always involve a moment of brute translation through which the singular experience of justice in one community is shaped into terms applicable to another, thus corrupting the original justice sensibility in order to suit the terms of the dominant culture (Derrida, 1992). For example, the Canadian government has formal-ised the aboriginal practice of 'circle sentencing' into the Canadian justice system, but has added Canadian lawyers and judges to the practice, ignoring the fact that these practices traditionally derived from aboriginal, rather than Canadian, state sovereignty. In this translated form, circle sentences may do more to reinforce Canadian legal hegemony than they do to bolster aboriginal traditional justice practices.

Based on the experiences of collectivities seeking to establish new models of justice that are subsequently corrupted by persistent structures of social power, one can understand why Derrida (1992) has gone so far as to declare justice an 'experience of the impossible'. By this, he means that justice, in its idealised sense, represents something that is always 'to come' rather than realisable in any immediate form—but he also acknowledges that we cannot simply abstain from the question of justice, because the demands of injustice are pressing. Therefore, he argues, we must attempt calculations of justice, but with the realisation that each calculation will be imperfect and must be open to future deconstructive criticism. These are, indeed, tenuous founda-tions on which to establish a sense of right and wrong.

In short, under present conditions, we are left with a view that justice is multiple, culturally particular and unrealisable in any full sense. In the realm of informal justice, we see these characteristics showing in a plurality of practitioner objectives. Thus, while a social justice orientation—that is, a view that informal justice should serve to meet the needs and improve the lives of community members—may direct the activity of some practitioners of informal justice, it is merely one orientation among many, because others will adhere to utilitarian or instrumentalist strategies designed to maximise collective or individual advantage. Moreover, while some informal justice practitioners may embrace a transformative orientation that sees personal and societal change as a goal of conflict resolution practices, other practitioners view informal justice more narrowly as a means for solving specific problems in a timely and efficient manner.

This leaves us with a difficult challenge in the remaining chapters. Our focus is on the *transformative* and social justice potential of informal justice, while we acknowledge that this is merely one form of informal justice and that these goals cannot be claimed to be the prime motivations of the informal justice movement as a whole. Thus, we necessarily acknowledge that ours is a partial analysis of informal justice that is most concerned with those forms of informal justice that claim an oppositional status in relation to the legal status quo, although we are also interested in how this oppositional strand relates to, influences and is influenced by competing informal justice approaches. It also raises the challenge that the transformative goals that we feel are important to informal justice are difficult to realise in a fragmented justice realm, particularly because there are several competing forms of informal justice more consonant with prevailing economic, political and social conditions. For this reason, our overarching purpose is to consider transformative informal justice as a political project directed toward defending informal justice from co-optation and dilution and toward creating new justice possibilities within a broader political-economic field of power.

An outline of the chapters to come

In the next chapter, we will clarify the concept of the informal–formal justice complex and offer an analytical framework for assessing the potential for collective empowerment to emerge from within this space. The two pillars of this framework are the work of Michel Foucault on 'governmentality', and the work of Jürgen Habermas on communicative action and discourse ethics. Proponents and critics of informal justice have drawn upon each author frequently; our objective is to appropriate insights from both scholars that will allow us to examine the transformative potential of informal justice.

Chapter 3 takes a closer look at civil mediation, paying specific attention to the role played by 'community mediation' in establishing a social justice agenda for informal justice. We will describe how this movement was co-opted by the state and legal professionals, and how mediation subsequently came to be a skill set applicable to countless types of conflict. This instrumentalisation of mediation has, to some extent, contributed to its role in bolstering, rather than opposing, dominant power relations. We will end the chapter with a consideration of mediation from the perspectives of both governmentality studies and discourse ethics, so that we can better articulate the contemporary perils and potentials of mediation within the informal–formal justice complex.

In Chapter 4, we provide an overview of the development of restorative justice as an 'informal' justice practice within the field of criminal law. In particular, we illustrate the growing divergences in restorative justice within the informal–formal justice complex, notably occurring over an emergent split between practitioners who work with government in an attempt to complement the criminal justice system (governmentalists) and practitioners who foreswear state involvement wherever possible (communitarians)—although a complete rejection of state involvement is difficult because both restorative justice types rely on state referrals and funding. Again using the work of Foucault and Habermas as in the last chapter, our aim is to demonstrate the conflicts and challenges that restorative justice faces within the informal–formal justice complex and in the current conjuncture of an expanding neoliberalism.

In Chapter 5, we show that, just as with mediation and restorative justice, the field of reparations politics is not unified. To date, reparations theorists tend to posit uniform, global trends to account for the rise of reparations politics. These trends include the notion of Barkan (2000) that we have entered a stage of neo-enlightenment in which group rights are gaining equal status to individual rights; Torpey (2001, borrowing from Fraser, 1997) suggests that reparations may be a product of 'post-Socialist' times in which subaltern groups lack a clear alternative to capitalism for articulating their dissatisfaction; Long and Brecke (2002) contend that the emotion work of conflict resolution is a product of an adaptive evolutionary psychology that ensures our continued survival; Novick (1999) offers the idea that a rising tide of Holocaust consciousness has led to an increase in reparations claims and arguments that point to the ascendancy of human rights discourses and their ability to reach even the farthest corners of the globe (Falk, 2000). Our contention is that there are diverse motivations driving the growth of reparative politics that range from the pursuit of repair as a means to societal transformation and justice, to its pursuit as a means of creating economic, political and legal stability (or 'certainty') within a specified region. Quite often, these ideal and pragmatic goals intersect, but in neoliberal times, greater emphasis has been placed upon achieving economic and governmental certainty through reparative processes. Nevertheless, our aim is to examine the goals and tactics of reparations politics within the informal–formal justice complex, and through the dual analytic lens of governmentality studies and communicative action theory, to assess whether or not reparations can promote societal transformation.

Finally, in our concluding chapter, we summarise the conditions of the informal–formal justice complex and the way in which these conditions limit the transformative potential of civil mediation, restorative justice and reparations. We also point, however, to empowering moments that may arise within the informal–formal justice complex. Informal justice practices do offer opportunities for resistance to domination; the challenge is to sustain this resistance so that it amounts to more than a fleeting disruption of the status quo. After exploring the various spaces from which a transformative informal justice might be launched, we use the notion of 'subaltern counter-publics' (Fraser, 1997) to describe how informal justice might seek both to withdraw from and to engage with the informal–formal justice system so as to present a prolonged challenge to its hegemony. In this sense, the fact that informal practices are not located outside the formal justice system, but are instead unavoidably constituted within it, signifies that it is both at risk of succumbing to the neoliberal influences that currently shape the parameters of the formal justice system *and* in a position to subvert those influences and reconfigure the culture and practice of justice to a more democratic and participatory form of governance.

Chapter 2

Assessing informal justice

In this chapter, we draw on the work of Michel Foucault and Jürgen Habermas to develop an analytical framework for assessing the informal–formal justice complex, a concept we adapt from the work of Garland and Sparks (2000) to describe the overlapping of formal and informal justice practices within the juridical field. We begin with a discussion of Foucault-inspired interventions into debates about informal justice, which challenge the claims of informal justice advocates as well as the state control view that informal justice is merely an extension of state power. This brings us to consider the field of governmentality studies, which deploys Foucault's neologism 'governmentality' to understand better the ways in which power operates through individual autonomy and choice, and not simply through the imposition of state-derived power. This latter perspective has added an important dimension to studies of informal justice by providing insight into the ways in which empowered participants in informal practices are nonetheless subject to (as well as subjects of) power. This critique is valuable in that it brings a more sophisticated understanding of power to our analyses of informal justice and initiates a discussion of the potential for disrupting domination. This perspective does, however, need to be accompanied by a broader political strategy for institutional change if it is to contribute to transformative juridical change.

To help us to evaluate the potential of informal justice as a political project, we then turn to Habermas' work on communicative rationality, the public sphere and discourse ethics, which allows us to begin an examination of the role that informal justice might play in reconstructed democratic processes designed to maximise deliberative engagement. Habermas' perspective also suffers from limitations in that, by envisioning the possibility of undistorted communication, it holds to an overly idealistic notion of interaction that does not fully account for the existence, in communicative settings, of the more subtle and less overt forms of power described by Foucault. In the end, we argue that insights from both Foucaultian and Habermasian perspectives will be necessary if we are to engage the political potential of informal justice.

Governmentality studies

In the early 1970s, French philosopher Michel Foucault turned his attention toward the question of power. He reasoned that:

> In order to conduct a concrete analysis of power relations, one would have to abandon the juridical model of sovereignty. That model assumes the individual as a subject of natural rights or original powers; it aims to account for the ideal genesis of the state; and it makes law the fundamental manifestation of power.
>
> (1994, p 59)

Through this statement, Foucault shifts emphasis from power as a mode through which individuals are dominated and controlled by centralised structures of law and government, to power as a set of techniques and relations through which the subject is produced. The latter emphasis permits an examination of micro-instances of power that do not arise through the machinations of powerful (class or state-based) actors, but which have significant effect on how we conduct our lives. For example, Foucault examined practices such as the Christian confessional to demonstrate how the subject, as an agent of power, actively participates in a project of self-creation by publicly identifying those aspects of self that most require change. As Foucault writes:

> Everyone in Christianity has the duty to explore who he is, what is happening within himself, the faults he may have committed, the temptations to which he is exposed. Moreover, everyone is obliged to tell these things to other people, and thus to bear witness against himself.
>
> (1994, p 178)

In this, we see a potent source of social power that operates through the complicit agency of the individual subject, who accepts the confessional not only as an opportunity for disciplinary penance, but also for self-directed reform.

This path of analysis eventually led Foucault to coin the term 'governmentality', which refers to 'a way of problematising life and seeking to act upon it' (Rose, 1993, p 288) in order to describe the sixteenth-century rise in arts of governance that were directed toward shaping the will and behaviour of individuals (Foucault, 1991; 1994). This governance occurs not simply through the might of the state, but rather through the proliferation of rationalities and modes of thought that non-coercively act as background assumptions guiding individual choices. That is, governance narrows the boundaries of what is thinkable so that our individual decisions fit within a limited set of normative options. Thus, the logic of rule takes shape within individual 'mentalities', and circumscribes thought and action, thereby effecting a 'responsibilisation corresponding to the new forms in which the governed are encouraged, freely and rationally, to conduct themselves' (Burchell, 1993, p 276).

Several scholars have taken up Foucault's conceptualisation of power and used it to intervene in discussions about informal justice. We will refer to this group as belonging to the field of 'governmentality studies', although they are elsewhere called the 'new informalists' (Matthews, 1988), a term that we find imprecise because some of these scholars are quite sceptical toward the notion of informalism. Indeed, much scholarship based on the work of Foucault—in particular, his later work on the *History of Sexuality* (1985; 1988; 1990) and his *Governmentality* lectures (1991)—suggests that the opposition between informal and formal justice is grossly overstated.

First, governmentality scholars criticise the informal–formal divide. They note that elements of the formal and the informal overlap, and are mutually reinforcing within the legal field (Fitzpatrick, 1995). For example, so-called informal practices, such as mediation and restorative justice, are argued to have clear formalistic elements, ranging from the scripts and interventions employed by mediators, to the subtle persuasive force used by actors in negotiation and meditation settings to encourage certain types of resolution from the parties in conflict. These practices are also said to rely heavily on formal definitions of law and crime, as well as on the formal system for referrals and funding, and on the threat of formal sanctions as motivation for encouraging participation in informal justice. Moreover, governmentality scholars suggest that informal and formal justice practices are not entirely separate, as is often assumed by those claiming to sit on one side or the other of the informal–formal divide. Indeed, there is a binary dependence that connects both justice forms, preventing us from understanding one without reference to the other. For example, the denigration of informal justice by state control critics as a 'second-class' form of justice merely reinforces the idea that there exists a 'first-class' mode of justice, which one would assume to be the courts. In other words, adversarial justice is conspicuously dominant only when there is reference to a marginalised form of 'alternative' justice. Similarly, if restorative justice were to replace the formal criminal justice system fully, it would lose its basis for self-definition, because so much of its identity relies on presenting itself as an 'alternative' to this system (Pavlich, 2005). Restorative justice defines itself as non-coercive rather than coercive, empowering rather than alienating, reintegrative rather than stigmatising, and so on, with the latter term in each pairing referencing the assumed conditions of formal justice. Defined as such, restorative justice becomes dependent on its referent —the criminal justice system—and it becomes difficult to imagine restorative justice separate from formal criminal justice.

Second, governmentality studies cast suspicion on the notion of autonomy that guides both the early informalist claims to social justice and the state control critique of informal justice. To suggest, as exponents of informal justice often do, that informal justice liberates citizens from state control or, conversely, that informal justice is a means for increasing social control, as do state control critics of informal justice, is to assume that it is possible to overcome completely the problems of coercion and power in social inter-action. But, according to governmentality studies, there is no space removed from power. In fact, the social freedom that is at stake in the debate is little more than a rationality of governance, because it is through enacting their freedom that citizens become responsibilised to decision-making practices consistent with particular forms of administrative rule (see Barry et al, 1996; Rose, 1999). In other words, we are provided with a semblance of autonomy when decisions are, in fact, made based upon a limited range of options; to be 'free', to make choices, assumes a specific mode of decision-making that draws on dominant modes of thinking, such as economic rationalities. So, while a participant in a restorative justice encounter may experience a sense of freedom and empowerment in helping to determine what remedial action an offender might take, that same participant may be less aware of how his reasoning is shaped by power. For instance, he may effortlessly incline toward cost-benefit and liberal-individualist modes of thought that make monetary restitution seem a natural remedy for the situation. Thus, although he osten-sibly offers his 'own' ideas within the restorative encounter, these ideas are built from a (neo)liberal social context that allows him to economise and individualise harm.

The notion that we require autonomy from state power also assumes that there exists a coherent locus of power that can be identified through the term 'state'. In contrast, governmentality scholars contend that governance stretches far beyond this singular institution (Rose, 1993) and can be found in everyday micro-societal contexts operating through the practices of local actors, far from the administrative calculations of state domination. In this sense, power does not simply emanate from a powerful state body that oppresses subordinate actors; instead, governmentality scholars suggest that power is often localised, productive and positive. In arguing that power can be positive, governmentality scholars do not claim that power is necessarily beneficial or useful; indeed, they strive to avoid such normative positions. Rather, they argue that power is creative; for example, mediation acts as a form of 'pastoral power' (Pavlich, 1996a) that serves to encourage individuals to construct new, non-disputing self-identities that are more amenable to governance. By learning conflict resolution skills, individuals engaged in mediation are also learning how better to manage their social behaviour. Similarly, critics have examined truth commissions, such as the South African Truth and Reconciliation Commission, and have found them complicit in cultivating quasi-religious and passive responses to brutal crimes through discourses of 'truth' and 'forgiveness', thereby denying victims the experi-ence of righteous anger and forcing upon them a 'compulsory compassion'

(Acorn, 2004). Power is therefore at work in informal justice settings, helping to produce non-combative and governable subjects and citizens.

Third, and following from the second point, governmentality scholars perceive informal justice as a mode of 'governmentality' or as a set of 'governmentalities' (Pavlich, 2005).[1] As noted above, for Foucault, governmentality refers to the manner in which the rationality of governance is distributed throughout society without the direction of a guiding hand to orchestrate its operation; instead, new 'mentalities' of governance are brought into the daily lives of individuals by experts, professionals and other persons who operate at arm's length from the state. Governmentality concerns itself with at least two practices: *techniques of discipline* and *technologies of the self*. With the former, governmentality creates 'normality' by constructing 'normal' individuals who are controlled, rather than coerced. For example, this may be achieved by dispersing therapeutic professionals into communities and having them guide individuals in the 'conduct of conduct', through models of psychological health that contribute to the normative reshaping of individual behaviour. With the latter, governmentality relies on citizens' own self-regulation as they come to internalise societal controls, and to play an active role in monitoring their own conduct and being responsible for their activities (Burchell, 1993; Pavlich, 1996a; 1996b). In Foucault's words, technologies of the self:

> permit individuals to effect by their own means, or with the help of others, a certain number of operations on their own bodies and souls, thoughts, conduct, and way of being, so as to transform themselves in order to attain a certain state of happiness, purity, wisdom, perfection or immortality.
>
> (1994, p 225)

This may be achieved through strategies that enjoin citizens to accept responsibility for their own governance, and to accept certain governmental rationalities as natural and unquestionable. Certain self-help programmes— Alcoholics Anonymous or anger management, for example—ask participants to police their own behaviour, so that they halt practices of drinking and emotional displays that are perceived to be socially unacceptable.

Both through techniques of discipline and technologies of self, governmentality ideally governs by encouraging or creating the conditions for reshaping the 'soul' or the conscience of the individual actor, rather than by utilising the oppressive mechanisms of the state. Informal justice allegedly qualifies as a form of governmentality, because it performs both of these tasks: it enlists a set of professionals and quasi-professionals (that is, conflict resolution specialists), as well as the individuals engaged in various conflicts,

---

1 The latter term recognises that there are diverse forms of informal justice.

into the project of governance 'at a distance' (Rose, 1993; 1996; Miller and Rose, 1990). Governance 'at a distance' entails the mobilisation of devices of governance that permit detachment between state power and localised forms of informal and self-governance. Thus, with informal justice, the state can retreat from some areas of justice provision, allowing informal justice providers and clients to spread the logic of rational governance. For instance, government support might be directed toward a community-based restorative justice agency, with the understanding that this group of quasi-professionals and volunteers will also attend to minor crimes committed by youth. This frees state resources from addressing this seemingly less serious social problem, while, at the same time, ensuring that prosocial governmentalities are spread among young people who might otherwise be inclined toward further disruptive behaviour.

Within these limits, the prospects for an 'alternative' and 'empowering' informal justice seem slim. First, any informal realm would appear to be predicated upon, and operate in relation to, the hegemonic force of formal law. Its transformative power is curtailed by its insertion in a legal framework entwined within the juridical logic of state and professional domination. For this reason, according to governmentality scholars, informal justice does not represent a true break from the 'formal'. Second, informal justice does not possess an adequate understanding of power and the limits of human autonomy, because it imagines communicative spaces free from the trappings of power—under the Foucaultian notion of power, this is impossible. Even if direct domination of one informal justice participant by another is prevented, more subtle and constitutive forms of power are still at work in the fashioning of non-disputive personalities through the technologies of informal justice. Finally, informal justice is itself embedded in the project of governance, through its promotion of informal justice governmentalities that are composed of specific techniques of discipline and technologies of the self. All of these factors combine to cast suspicion on informal justice claims to represent an 'alternative' to a formal and oppressive system of legal governance. This is not to suggest, however, that the work of Foucault, or of governmentality scholars, leaves no options for challenging the juridical status quo. Indeed, a critical ethos, or reflexive mode of 'care of the self', is prescribed by Foucault (1994) as a means of encouraging awareness of moments of domination, so that disruptive behaviours might be fashioned to lessen the brunt of governing patterns of power.

Perhaps because governmentality studies appears, on first glance, so decidedly opposed to informal justice, informal justice proponents have spent little time engaging with the critical ironies illuminated by this perspective; nor have they yet adopted a countering perspective able to provide a theoretical justification for their practices in light of these criticisms. Indeed, as we will argue below, much of the informal justice literature lacks a solid theoretical foundation. For this reason, we draw on the work of Jürgen

Habermas, only now beginning to find supporters among conflict resolution proponents (see Augusti-Panareda, 2005; Chilton and Cuzzo, 2005; Dzur and Olson, 2004; Parkinson and Roche, 2004), in order to provide conceptual support for, and guidance to, the practices of informal conflict resolution.

Communicative rationality and discourse ethics

There is much that can be found in Habermas' work that might serve as a theoretical base for informal justice practice. Habermas, as a student and then member of the Frankfurt School of Critical Theory (see Jay, 1973), shifted away from the crippling notion of an omnipresent instrumental reason that marked the work of his philosophical forebears (Horkheimer and Adorno, 1976), who believed that actors in the contemporary world suffer from a 'lack of critical distance' that inescapably entwines them in the strategic rationalities of capitalism. In contrast, Habermas appropriated insights from the 'linguistic turn', seeing in communication the possibility for ethical, non-strategic human interaction. This communicative rationality involves the use of language toward achieving common objectives and normative understandings among parties in conversation. First, subjects participating in interaction would require a certain level of linguistic competence and psychological maturity in order to communicate effectively, responsibly and in a reciprocal manner. Second, specific ground rules of communicative interaction would be necessary to ensure fair and uncoerced communication. Habermas lists these communicative presuppositions as follows:

1. Every subject with the competence to speak and act is allowed to take part in discourse.
2. a) Everyone is allowed to question any assertion whatever, b) everyone is allowed to introduce any assertion whatever into the discourse, c) everyone is allowed to express his attitudes, desires and needs.
3. No speaker may be prevented by internal or external coercion from expressing his rights as laid down in (1) and (2).

(1990, p 89)

These a priori rules are thus intended to ensure that communication does not fall victim to instrumental and strategic motivations. The aforementioned grounding 'universal core' out of which these rules emanate is a notion of argumentation, which serves as a universal procedural form. Argumentation fits this role, because even those who argue against the possibility of there being universal normative standards must engage in argumentation. In so doing, they assume that certain pragmatic presuppositions of communication are in place, allowing them to employ reason and rationality in an attempt to convince others that their arguments are sound (Habermas, 1990). In this manner, they engage in what Habermas, borrowing from the work of

Karl Otto Apel (1987), refers to as a 'performative contradiction'. In other words, those who doubt that argumentation is a procedural universal often verify the position they intend to discount by employing argumentative reason to disprove the universality of argumentation. Thus, because rational argument is a necessary element in any discussion of norms, for Habermas, it is upon this basis that a moral procedure of justice can be developed. Habermas therefore takes the following statement as the 'weak' universal on which the process of discourse ethics can be built: 'only those norms can claim to be valid that meet (or could meet) with the approval of all affected in their capacity as participants in a practical discourse [or rational argument]' (Habermas, 1990, p 66).

Such uncoerced discourse is the basis for what Habermas calls the 'ideal speech situation', which refers to social conditions that allow for equality and autonomy among participants in discourse, and follows the guidelines for discourse ethics outlined above. If social conditions permit individuals to deliberate freely according to the presuppositions of communication, then we have before us a discussion that approximates the ideal speech situation. It should, however, be noted that, for Habermas, the ideal speech situation does not refer to an actual 'situation', because these ideal conditions are very difficult to realise in a world rife with power and instrumentalising tendencies; rather, the ideal speech situation refers to an analytical ideal against which actual discourses can be measured. The more we seek to emulate this situation in our public communication, the more likely we are to establish deliberative conditions that allow for the fair consideration of normative questions.

Another evaluative standard for assessing the adequacy of communicative action rests in what Habermas calls 'validity claims'. Such claims typically operate as the bedrock of our everyday conversations in that we assume that statements we make to others are being treated as valid; otherwise, we would be asked to defend them. For Habermas, there are four types of culturally invariant validity claim that are in play when we converse. Communication is inhibited when one or more of these claims is challenged and fails to obtain agreement:

1. 'Comprehensibility'—(What do you mean?)—the speakers use language adequately enough to be understood; the speech-act is intelligible to participants.
2. 'Truth'—(Is what you say true?)—the statements (utterances) of speakers adequately portray realities in relation to the objective world; the speaker is offering reliable knowledge; the speech-act is factually correct.
3. 'Rightness'—(Are you entitled to say that?)—the statements of speakers are appropriate or legitimate in a given situation in relation to shared norms and values; the statements seem right and proper and can be assimilated by participants.

4. 'Truthfulness'—(Do you really mean it?)—the statements of speakers are sincere and authentic in the expression of intentions and feelings; the statements are veracious and not intended to deceive participants

(Ratner, 2007)

If the communicative conditions of discourse ethics are in place, these validity claims can be discussed openly and equitably.

Ideally, in democratic contexts, all of these conditions would also define interactions within what Habermas (1989) calls the 'public sphere'. The public sphere is a notion that Habermas draws from his study of eighteenth-century bourgeois public discussions in which reason would occasionally triumph over raw power. While Habermas is realistic about the limitations of this public sphere, he also sees in it the potential for establishing a model for public reflection. Thus, for Habermas, the notion of the public sphere refers to those domains of public deliberation outside of formal state institutions. The public sphere provides a setting in which validity claims can be contested openly for purposes of reaching consensus on general normative and political questions that face members of particular societal aggregations.

One can see, in all of the above concepts, a theoretical approach that provides rational grounding for key practices of informal justice, because many proponents of informal justice also place a premium on unfettered communication between rational and open-minded agents (see, for example, Braithwaite, 2002; Bush and Folger, 1994). Just as in the guidelines for discourse ethics, informal justice proponents claim that all parties must be permitted to speak and to bring into the discussion matters they feel to be relevant. Facilitators of informal justice are also instructed to neutralise or to challenge all noticeable attempts at coercion so that rational discourse can prevail. In this sense, the goal of many types of informal justice, as in the ideal speech situation, is to create communicative settings in which validity claims can be made and challenged through a deliberative discourse directed toward achieving consensus. Speakers within informal justice contexts are asked to speak sincerely ('Truthfulness') and honestly ('Truth') about what transpired, to clarify their sentiments so that they are understandable for their co-disputants ('Comprehensibility'), and to respect shared norms of mutual acknowledgement and dignity ('Rightness'). Any claim that violates these requirements is likely to be subject to argument. Finally, it might also be suggested that many informal justice settings fit the description of a Habermasian public sphere, because they are ostensibly located outside of the state and the formal legal system, allowing for public discursive engagement with issues of justice.

When coupled with Habermas' theory of communicative action and dis-course ethics, informal justice's emphasis on communication ideally comes to be guided by a pragmatic and clear procedural ethic directed toward mutual growth and understanding. Too often, theories of informal justice are based upon unspoken presuppositions about the conciliatory nature of human interaction. In some cases, this is embedded in a sketchy anthropological narrative that recreates a peaceable past in which actors worked their conflicts out, before the state intervened to disrupt this natural communal capacity. Theoretically speaking, this is a shaky ethical foundation for informal justice practices because it rests too much upon the authority of the past rather than on providing a strong moral or ethical rationale for current practice. Moreover, basing informal justice on unfounded assumptions about human nature and other imagined pasts leaves this form of justice susceptible to appropriation by social and political forces seeking to use these practices for their own purposes. This risk of appropriation stems from the fact that these arbitrary assumptions deny informal justice a philosophically grounded, normative procedural model against which to check the application of its practices in the real world.

Indeed, in earlier versions of Habermas' theory, we can see clear warnings of the dangers of instrumental appropriation of practices such as informal justice in the distinction he draws between 'system' and 'lifeworld'.[2] To understand these dangers, we must first understand the communicative conditions of the lifeworld. The lifeworld is:

> . . . formed from more or less diffuse, always unproblematic, background convictions. This lifeworld background serves as a source of situation definitions that are presupposed by participants as unproblematic. In their interpretive accomplishments the members of a communication community demarcate the one objective world and their intersubjectively shared social world from the subjective world of individuals and (other) collectives.
>
> (Habermas, 1984, p 70)

This is the space of communicative action in which reciprocity, consensus and similar communicative goals can flourish. It is also the space in which one would imagine are located the 'communities of care' (that is, communities formed by people who share personal relationships with one another), as discussed by practitioners and theorists of informal justice (see McCold and Wachtel, 1998). This communicative space is, however, at risk of colonisation by the system, where the delinguistified steering media of power and money ensure the dominance of instrumental reason. More and more, these instrumental logics force their way into lifeworld spaces, transforming

---

2 'System' refers to the forces of production and the impersonal 'steering mechanisms' of money and power ('delinguistified media') pervading late capitalist society, whereas 'lifeworld' refers to the shared cultural conventions, linguistic stock and communicative interactions of people in their everyday social contexts.

communicative practices into self-interested and economic competitions. The danger of colonisation often coincides with what Habermas refers to as 'juridification', meaning the entry of a greater degree of legal regulation into the lifeworld. Indeed, some socio-legal scholars have worried that informal justice might itself contribute to the greater juridification and colonisation of the lifeworld (see Brooker, 1999; Langer, 1998) by bringing the force of formal law more directly into communities rather than representing a form of justice that is ideally suited to these lifeworld spaces. Therefore, for Habermas, there is always the threat that power and instrumental reasoning will invade and occupy the space of the lifeworld. For this reason, we need to establish pragmatic universal standards through which we can identify these incursions, and counter their tendency to distort communication and distract subjects from the goal of mutual understanding.

In Habermas' later works, such as *Between Facts and Norms* (1999), he suggests that colonisation and juridification are not the necessary and inevitable results of attempts to connect institutions of governance with deliberative publics. Instead, Habermas seeks to take a 'reconstructive' approach to democratic institutions to illustrate how they can still serve emancipatory purposes so long as they provide channels for meaningful public input. In other words, Habermas does not assume that current formal institutions need to be torn asunder in order to recover democratic practices; rather, he:

> accepts that administrative and market systems are inseparable parts of today's complex societies, but contends that they should be opened to the influence of the will of the public through informal procedures of deliberation, as formal outside governmental bodies.
>
> (Shabani, 2003, p 94)

In this sense, Habermas suggests that there are palpable opportunities for democratic practice through which public actors can affect the world around them. What is needed is a means to connect public deliberations with administrative institutions. The legal realm takes on crucial significance in Habermas' thinking, because it represents a space between system and lifeworld that can absorb discursively formed matters of public opinion; it acts as an institutional bridge, allowing cultural and political thoughts developed in the lifeworld to cross over and challenge, or modify, the instrumentality of the system (see Habermas, 1999). Following this line of reasoning, the relationship between formal law and informal deliberative practices is not in, and of itself, problematic, so long as opportunities are available for informal justice to have an impact on formal justice and, therefore, the system. If this relationship lacks reciprocity, then we are more likely to see hegemonic incursions into informal justice and the lifeworld, as suggested through the notions of colonisation and juridification. Ideally, however, informal justice practices could take on the character of 'informal public spheres', in which participatory discourses on justice and conflict might take place, and through which citizens might mobilise opposition to systems of power and domination through the force of collective communicative action that attains the sanctity of law.

This brings us back to the issue of how informal justice processes might act as informal public spheres. We are not suggesting informal justice, as it currently exists, fully meets the criteria of the ideal speech situation or even of a public sphere. As we noted above, however, many informal justice practitioners do attempt to implement ground rules similar to those suggested by Habermas, even if they do not derive directly from the theory of communicative action. To clarify this claim, brief examples from mediation, restorative justice and reparations are in order.

Mediators will often meet individually with the parties to the conflict to ensure that they are aware of the rules for the mediation game. Especially for those we refer to in the next chapter as 'facilitative' mediators, it is important that the parties know that they are free to raise any issue they so desire, but it is also crucial that they do not interrupt and that they do not respond in an aggressive manner to their co-disputant(s). The mediator will further remind the parties of these rules immediately prior to the mediation session. In addition, the mediator will use a series of cues to encourage the parties to continue to abide by the rules of the game as the mediation progresses. These include 'reframing' techniques, whereby the mediator will translate an adversarial statement into more neutral terms, and 'summarising', which allows the mediator to restate a series of issues in more straightforward and communicable terms (Picard, 1998; see also Woolford and Ratner, 2007).

These techniques are also not uncommon in restorative justice encounters and reparations negotiations, although these disputes might possess even greater potential for animosity and discord because they touch on matters of a criminal nature. Nonetheless, it is the case with all three of these practices that they can act as a form of public sphere in which normative questions pertaining to civil and criminal law, as well as the broader social conditions underlying alleged injustices, can be subject to deliberative discussion. Restorative justice encounters, if they involve community members in addition to the victim and offender,[3] are occasions in which multiple concerns about the particular case, but also broader concerns about community conditions and community safety, can be voiced and debated. Similarly, truth commissions often provide the opportunity for victims, perpetrators, experts and bystanders to offer their perspectives on the harms caused by a previous regime or non-governmental militias (Hayner, 2002). Such discussion not only allows for the clarification of past events, but also enables citizens to

---

3 Our use of terms such as 'victim', 'offender', 'perpetrator' and 'bystander' should not be taken as an unquestioned acceptance of these purported identities. We recognise that, in actual situations of crime and mass violence, these identities often overlap in complex fashion.

collectively begin the process of redefining the future. How do they wish to live together? What values might bind them together as a political community? Thus, in all three types of informal justice, efforts are made to establish conditions that facilitate open and fair discussion of normative matters among community members.

Habermas' theory of communicative action and discourse ethics is not, however, in all respects, an ideal framework for interpreting informal justice. Habermas' insistence that participants suspend their particularistic lifeworld concerns when they enter into communicative action contradicts the belief, common among informal justice practitioners, that the specificity of the conflict situation should determine the form taken by the dispute resolution process.[4] Furthermore, Habermas' commitment to establishing a universal core in the form of argumentation to guide the process of discourse ethics also has the potential to clash with the flexibility touted by practitioners as a key aspect of informal justice.[5] Finally, Habermas' rationalistic approach to discourse may seem unappealing to some exponents of informal justice, who see purpose in emotionally charged discussions within which passions, rather than reason, are at the fore.

Habermas' (1999, p 56) vision of law as a '*hinge*' between system and lifeworld has also been criticised for assuming that the formal institutional infrastructure can be redeemed and turned toward radical democratic ends (Lee, 1998; Shabani, 2003). Governmentality scholars would also question whether undominated discursive spaces could ever be created that would then spread their influence to the 'system'.[6] For these scholars, it would be more fruitful to explore the fullness of power relations, in order to discover fissures and opportunities for resistance and disruption, rather than to rely upon democratic institutions to channel oppositional public opinion. Reflecting on Habermas' work, Foucault writes:

> I am quite interested in his work, although I know he completely disagrees with my views. . . . I have always had a problem insofar as he gives communicative relations this place which is so important and, above all, a function that I would call 'utopian'. The idea that there could exist a

---

4 In his early work, Habermas suggested that the particular 'lifeworld' concerns of participants in discourse ethics need to be bracketed so that the procedure could focus on building consensus. In his later works, however, Habermas clarifies that, in some cases, particularities must be addressed through the assessment of the 'appropriateness' of the communicative decision to the particular situation (see Shabani, 2003).

5 It should be noted, however, that Habermas describes this as a 'weak' universal that simply speaks to the basic presumptions of communicative interaction.

6 They would also very likely find the notion of 'system' problematic, because it suggests a coherence and orchestration of power that scholars of governmentality studies argue is neither likely, nor empirically valid.

state of communication that would allow games of truth to circulate freely without any constraints or coercive effects, seems utopian to me. This is precisely a failure to see that power relations are not something that is bad in itself ... I do not think that a society can exist without power relations, if by that one means the strategies by which individuals try to direct and control the conduct of others. The problem, then, is not to try to dissolve them in the utopia of completely transparent communication but to acquire the rules of law, the management techniques, and also the morality, the *ēthos*, the practice of the self, that will allow us to play these games of power with as little domination as possible.

(1994, p 298)

Thus, according to this view, there is no power-free space in which deliberation can occur free of constraint. The goal is to minimise and destabilise those forms of power that are particularly invidious—namely, domination.

In addition, governmentality scholars view Habermas as locked within the same antinomical struggle that troubled the state control critique of informal justice; namely, Habermas maintains an opposition between freedom and domination that, according to proponents of governmentality studies, is unsustainable (Barry et al, 1996, pp 12–13). For them, power intersects with our acts of freedom, making it difficult to envision a non-coercive communicative space (Rose, 1996). For instance, even in freely choosing to mediate rather than to litigate a conflict, we are engaging in a project of working upon ourselves, acknowledging that conflict is disruptive and counterproductive, and seeking to redirect the conflict toward conciliatory and accommodative ends.

In the next section of this chapter, we seek to examine more closely the space of informal justice, to begin to assess whether the critical and reflexive ethos suggested by governmentality studies as a response to the pervasiveness of power can be harnessed to a pragmatic Habermasian strategy that seeks to foster empowered communication, and to identify institutional paths toward social transformation.

Dilemmas facing informal justice: the informal–formal justice complex

Governmentality scholars, as we have noted, question the informal–formal and alternative–complement divides. Given their critique of informal justice, one might speak instead of there being an *informal–formal justice complex*. This term, adapted from Garland and Sparks (2000, p 199), describes the cultural, economic and political relations within the juridical field through which adversarial/punitive and conciliatory/restorative justice forms coexist and reinforce one another, despite their apparent competition. Indeed, it is their seeming contradiction that allows them to operate as opposite poles of the juridical field, locating all justice forms within their intermediary space. Thus, the informal and the formal are crucially intertwined, but this is not to suggest that justice programmes are all equally beholden to the limitations of the informal–formal justice complex. Those programmes that claim to be 'informal', which seek to foster communicative space for open and honest discussion of social conflicts, may hold potential for disrupting the boundaries of this complex. This potential can, however, only be realised if practitioners of informal justice are able to facilitate discussions that are guided by a degree of reflexive engagement, enabling them to challenge imposed or taken-for-granted hegemonic (neoliberal) scripts; in other words, they must promote a critical ethos within interactive informal justice settings that stimulates greater awareness of the dangers of various forms of domination (social, cultural, political and professional). In this sense, we believe that internal and strategic efforts to destabilise the informal–formal justice complex are possible.

But before we explore this potential, we must first describe the broader context within which the juridical field is situated: namely, the conditions of the contemporary juridical field in an overarching neoliberalism.

The 'juridical field' is defined by systems of vision and division, dispositions, and schemata of perception and judgement that orient those who operate within and upon its governing structures. In Bourdieu's words:

> The juridical field is the site of competition for monopoly of the right to determine the law. Within this field there occurs a confrontation among actors possessing a technical competence which is inevitably social and which consists essentially in the socially recognised capacity to interpret a corpus of texts sanctifying a correct or legitimised vision of the social world.
>
> (1987, p 817)

Thus, conflicts are understood within the juridical field through a lens that 'converts them into juridical confrontations' (Bourdieu, 1987, p 832). In this manner, the juridical field is permeated by dominant logics that structure thought and action in juridical terms. In terms of the informal–formal justice complex, this makes it very difficult to think of, or to enact, justice in a manner contrary to pervasive juridical norms, including those that serve the reproduction of domination within the juridical field (by legal professionals) and within the broader social field (by powerful actors or forces). Therefore, even those justice practices that are marginalised within the juridical field have difficulty breaking free from dominant power relations and tend to draw on legal rationalities in their attempts to create alternative justice practices.

The dominance of juridical reasoning serves the interests of those who possess higher levels of juridical capital or legal competence and thereby provides these actors with a better 'feel for the game' within the juridical field. This translates into greater juridical power for legal professionals, who are the authorised interpreters of legal codes. It also amounts to a greater sense of alienation and disempowerment among everyday persons who lack formal legal training or experience. This imbalance of juridical competence represents the cultural side of the juridical field, which creates the conditions for professional domination of both formal and informal justice practices—but this field also contributes to the reproduction of political and economic systems of domination. In other words, the juridical field overlaps with, and reinforces, other fields of social power and is therefore also influenced by reigning logics of domination within the economic or political fields; it can even play a role in reinforcing and protecting the power of dominant economic and political actors. In this analysis, we will use the term 'neoliberalism' to describe the economic and political framework that we believe has the greatest current influence on the informal–formal justice complex.

Neoliberalism is both a political and economic philosophy. As an economic philosophy, neoliberalism operates by opening markets to trade, by encouraging deregulation, decentralisation and flexibilisation, and, in general, by weakening collective structures that possess the potential to obstruct the free flow of capital (for example, the state). As a political philosophy, neoliberalism promotes and deploys governmentalities that are designed to increase citizen self-sufficiency and to free state resources from previous welfare state commitments. Indeed, 'neoliberalism' is the term that governmentality scholars often give to current political conditions defined by a confluence of techniques of discipline, technologies of self, responsibilisation and governance at a distance.

Under these juridical and neoliberal conditions, certain dangers exist for justice practices that aspire toward informal standards. Locked within the informal–formal justice complex, informal justice is susceptible to the broader pressures that are operational within the juridical field—pressures that tend toward reproducing the dominance of legal professionals and toward encouraging the instrumental use of informal justice practices to achieve specific (that is, neoliberal) economic and governance goals. To name but a few of these pressures, they include attempts to develop systems of mediator accreditation and professionalisation; government funding practices that require restorative justice agencies to compete in quasi-market conditions for operating resources, and efforts to direct reparative processes toward results that are complementary to state and corporate economic goals, rather than toward justice for victims. These and other tendencies entail the dilution of the social justice discourse that once motivated the informal justice movement, a discourse that governments typically view as impracticable. Instead, they harness the participatory programmes of informal justice to the cause of furthering neoliberal penetration into the social world.

A response to the socio-political context of neoliberalism informed by governmentality studies would suggest a different justice—one that works to subvert and destabilise the informal–formal justice complex—to deconstruct the assumptions of formal law and disrupt the binary relationship between formal law and informal justice. Such attempts to rethink justice outside the limitations of the dominant juridical order help us to imagine new justice possibilities and to provide the critical ethos necessary for interrogating persistent power relations. Moreover, they suggest the cultivation of new dispositions, or reflexive technologies of self, that would disrupt impositions of power and open fissures through which new potentials for action and thought might emerge.

These suggestions do, however, need to be more clearly channelled toward pragmatic political engagements. As Hinkson (1998, p 122) notes, governmentality scholars often 'seem unable to contribute towards a politics which is anything more than a reflection of neo-liberal circumstances'. In other words, the message to engage, for example, in a destabilising governance of the self when faced with the constraints of contemporary economic life becomes little more than the progressive flipside to neoliberal responsibilisation—each individual remains charged with the task of extending his or her own freedom from domination—unless we can find a means to direct this critical sensibility toward collective action.

The governmentality studies' critique of informal justice also needs to address more fully the range of informal practices at work within the juridical field: mediators' techniques vary from evaluative, to facilitative, to transformative; restorative justice programmes vary in respect of how tied they are to the state; reparations serve an array of purposes, ranging from societal transformation, to societal reconciliation, to establishing more stable economic relations. While governmentality scholars help us to understand how power operates in these multiple informal justice sites, they have (to date) offered an insufficient basis for evaluating the varying political potential of these divergent practices.

Indeed, governmentality exponents often leave us stranded through their theoretical refusal to offer political and institutional options for initiating change. This is characteristic of other 'post-structuralist' approaches to the problem of informal justice, such as Jacques Derrida-inspired perspectives that call for a vigilant deconstruction of all justice forms in a continual search for a justice that is always 'to come' (Derrida, 1992; see also Pavlich, 2001; 2005). While these perspectives provide compelling criticisms of the many oversights and problematic claims of informal justice, they also prematurely annul the efforts of informal justice practitioners. That is, although the informal–formal justice complex suggests an infinite looping of formal and informal processes in a self-reinforcing stasis, and a persistent, overarching juridical logic imbricated in the relations of ruling, there may well be opportunities for resistance and change within this seemingly closed system

—resistances that begin with a collective effort to create the sort of disruptions and fissures recommended by Foucault and governmentality scholars.

The counter-hegemonic impulses that guide these resistances, if properly channelled within informal venues, could be developed into efforts to explore these disruptions and fissures in concert. In this sense, a radical practice of informal justice would encourage disruptive critical engagements, transforming informal encounters into a phenomenological assault on existing conventions of juridical and neoliberal domination. But even if informal justice encounters are able to provoke criticism and creativity among participants, a means is still needed for enabling the outcomes of informal encounters to have an impact on social policy and legislation; otherwise, this critical energy may prove nothing more than a momentary and fleeting resistance to the prevailing order. It is in overcoming this sense of impotent marginalisation that Habermas' work on communicative action and the public sphere is most helpful. Through Habermas, we begin to see how, assuming that the ground-level presuppositions of discourse ethics are put into place and that democratic institutions are reconstructed to better serve deliberative public engagement, communicative action might be converted into efficacious political and collective action.

It must be acknowledged, however, that the Habermasian attempt to discern ideal communicative conditions though which public discussion might influence the structures of power faces several challenges that we will address in Chapter 6. First, Habermas' notion of the public sphere has been roundly criticised for ignoring the power imbalances and exclusions upon which the traditional public sphere has been based (Benhabib, 1992; Fraser, 1992). Furthermore, Habermas does not sufficiently problematise the degree to which the public sphere in capitalist democracies serves as the ground upon which consent for the hegemonic order is established: political world views are narrowed and limited to those made available for public dissemination (Crossley, 2004). Second, Habermas overestimates the mediating role played by law as a bridge between system and lifeworld. As governmentality studies suggests, the law is deeply embedded in the field of social power, assisting in its wider diffusion. Finally, Habermas' perspective, especially that which arises in *Between Facts and Norms* (1999), appears conservative, in the sense that it is unclear how social transformation can occur when the influence of public discourse is dependent upon existing democratic institutions of law and government, which are themselves hegemonically inundated (Shabani, 2003).

Situated within the informal–formal justice complex and more broadly within the juridical field, how can a counter-hegemonic justice measure mobilise dissent and sunder the current juridical configuration of professional power and neoliberal dominance? From the standpoint of governmentality studies, disruptive activities are needed to allow us to practise informal justice with 'as little domination as possible' (Foucault, 1994, p 44). From the standpoint of communicative action and discourse ethics, opportunities for deliberative interactions that are disinterred from existing normative sediments and directed toward institutional change must be facilitated. We suggest that, although each of these theories contains contradictory elements, each one can contribute to an understanding of how a space can be created for the exercise of a counter-hegemonic 'informal' justice. In our following discussions of mediation, restorative justice and reparations, we heed the theoretical strictures posed by governmentality scholars without discarding the democratic potential of informal justice practices operating from a place within the informal–formal justice complex.

Conclusion

As we enter our detailed discussion of specific forms of so-called informal justice, it is important to keep in mind several points touched upon in the first two chapters, as follows.

- Informal justice is a contested term: there is no longer, if there ever was, a 'pure' informal justice that is entirely separate from formal systems of law.
- Informal and formal justices are necessarily entwined, forming what we term an 'informal–formal justice complex' of mutually reinforcing justice relations.
- The informal–formal justice complex is itself situated within the broader juridical field and influenced by societal transformations, including the shift from Keynesianism to neoliberalism and globalisation.
- Governmentality studies and discourse ethics are described here as theoretical perspectives that make distinct, but complementary, contributions to our understanding of 'informal justice'. While we agree with the thrust of the governmentality studies' critique of informal justice and appreciate the critical potential of a reflexive ethos informed by these concerns, we also believe that a political strategy is needed to allow alternative justice movements to translate this critical ethos into political action, and to bring about change in democratic and institutional patterns at a broader societal level. For the latter project, we see promise in the Habermasian model of discourse ethics, in that it offers a pragmatic and institutionally grounded vision of democratic reconstruction.

Civil mediation, our focus for Chapter 3, represents a difficult challenge in respect of these points, because it is perhaps more embedded in the culture and practices of the informal–formal justice complexes than are the other justice procedures we discuss.

Chapter 3

Mediation in the informal– formal justice complex

Mediation, at its most basic level, is a practice in which an impartial facilitator intervenes to assist parties in resolving a conflict. In this chapter, we trace the history of this conflict resolution practice. In so doing, we demonstrate that the evolution of mediation follows a jagged path, beginning as a community-based practice, but breaking into a variety of legal, business and social justice-based models. This multiform development requires an assessment of mediation that is sensitive to its varied and contradictory forms. In this regard, we situate mediation within the informal–formal justice complex so as to highlight both its susceptibility to co-optation, owing to its immersion in the hegemonic field of law, and its potential for generating oppositional ideas and practices.

It should be noted at the outset, however, that we are focused here on what we term 'civil mediation', by which we mean facilitative practices that deal with local, non-criminal disputes. Mediation, as a conflict resolution skill or technique, is not solely used in civil cases—it is also employed in restorative justice and reparations, the subjects of our next two chapters—but it has followed a distinct path of development in the realm of civil law, within which it has been more actively incorporated into formal practices of law and more formalised as a professional practice. Not all forms of civil mediation have taken this route, however. Particular attention will be paid here to what has been called 'community mediation' (also sometimes termed 'neighbourhood' or 'popular' justice), because it is this subcategory of mediation practice that is most dedicated to the project of social justice. It bills itself as more than a mere 'add-on' that improves the efficiency and functionality of the formal justice system; rather, the primary aim of community mediation is to promote community autonomy, empowerment and harmony.

A brief history of mediation

Ancient roots?

Mediation has a long history as a communal form of dispute resolution. In small-scale and kinship-based societies, community solidarity had to be maintained to ensure collective survival. Transgressions against communal norms were perceived as serious threats. In instances of norm violation and conflict, it was crucial that the community intervene to rectify disputes and to ensure communal harmony. Within these social settings, the aforementioned distinction between 'civil' and 'criminal' disputes had no meaning, because these terms refer to state-derived definitions of wrongdoing. All was simply 'conflict' and 'disruption', and, while some conflicts were considered more serious, they all required communal attention for the sake of maintaining social stability. Conflict resolution interventions, as noted in Chapter 1, took a variety of forms—some punitive; others conciliatory—but a common tactic was to have a respected community member, who was known to the disputing parties, intervene to help to establish a mutually acceptable resolution (Michalowski, 1985).

When tracing the history of mediation, however, there is an unfortunate tendency to reach back into diverse cultural milieux, and to claim a definite continuity between justice practices in these small-scale communities and modern forms of mediation. This often results in reductive comparisons that remove culturally distinct justice forms from their historical contexts, ignoring the historical changes that have reshaped mediation and its relationship to the informal–formal justice complex. It is therefore important to keep in mind that small-scale mediation occurred in communities defined by high levels of shared beliefs and normative agreement. There was also a high degree of interdependency and common goals that shaped societal interactions. Additionally, these practices were not secondary to a more powerful formal juridical system, but instead represented the dominant forms of societal governance (Kueneman, 2004). In contemporary pluralistic societies, few of these conditions remain, except perhaps in retreatist micro-communities that actively maintain a distance from the mainstream (for example, some Mennonite communities). But even such micro-communities are not completely removed from the reach of law and may find themselves embroiled within the formal juridical system over issues ranging from taxation to criminal matters.

Attempts to imagine a foundational and historical mediation practice as the basis for modern mediation distract researchers from recognising the full complexity of mediation's development and transformation. The societal context in which mediation operates has changed so dramatically that attempts to recover a supposed 'golden age' of mediated justice are misdirected. Two key factors to consider in this respect are the emergence of the centralised state and that of the capitalist economic system.

With regards to the former, we can roughly trace the Western origins of conflict between formal and informal justice systems to the twelfth century, at which time increasingly powerful European kings sought to extend their control throughout their claimed national regions, doing away with pockets of non-state regulation. This entailed the entry of law into local contexts, which was, in many cases, perceived by citizens as a state-directed imposition upon their privacy and autonomy. One vehicle for this entry, in the British context, was the Crown's support for merchant law and its assistance in enforcing the rules of commerce. Through this initiative, the state successfully extended its control and helped to stabilise commercial conditions (Kueneman, 2004). Thus, formal law made an aggressive entry into everyday life, and the state's role as an overseer and arbiter of justice is a consequence of this incursion that many advocates of informal justice still view in terms of the state 'stealing' conflict from communities (Christie, 1977).

This initial state effort combined with the emergent interests of a class of legal professionals who worked to broaden the legal domain to include a greater variety of matters and communities. With the state extending its reach across national domains, the opportunity arose to expand and consolidate the legal monopoly over conflict resolution. Moreover, social changes, such as urbanisation and industrialisation, added to the complexity of modern life, creating conditions in which recourse to 'neutrals' trained in the law appeared more rational: societal bonds were no longer strong enough to permit informal modes of negotiated justice. These were, indeed, fortuitous times for legal professionals, who were primed to play an even larger role in the administration of justice and the regulation of capitalist commerce.

This double movement of state centralisation and legal professional monopolisation continued during the early development of Western liberal democracies, as can be observed in the experiences of nation building in the American colonies. In the seventeenth and eighteenth centuries, religious communities such as the Puritans and the Quakers sought to preserve conflict resolution practices that they viewed as more consistent with their spiritual beliefs: namely, community-mediated problem solving, rather than recourse to the formal law. Indeed, the law was often viewed as an intrusive and disruptive force that threatened community harmony—but this view began to change as internal differences emerged and shifted community life toward greater pluralism. As colonial towns and cities became more diverse, communities could not continue to rely on shared norms and values as the bedrock for informal justice practices; instead, relations became more competitive and therefore better suited to the adversarial standards of the courts (Auerbach, 1983). These disruptive influences provided an opportunity for the state to intervene and for legal professionals to service disputes within these communities.

The impact of the diversification of communal life on local justice practices, as described above, raises the question of whether or not mediation can survive in the complex modern world. But this question confuses mediation as a situated cultural practice with mediation as a conflict resolution technique. With regard to the former, the practice of mediation is embedded within a specific cultural cosmology that provides the practice with an underlying logic that resonates with shared community norms. In this context, mediation is a seemingly natural and often habitual response to community strife. In contrast, mediation as a conflict resolution technique situates mediation as one among many legal practices that can be drawn upon in appropriate circumstances. This is why some contemporary mediators refer to mediation as a form of 'appropriate dispute resolution' rather than 'alternative dispute resolution', because what they offer is a system supplement rather than replacement. This is the spirit in which Lon Fuller (1971) hails the practice, in his seminal article on mediation. Fuller notes that mediation is more appropriate to 'polycentric' disputes: that is, disputes that involve multiple parties and multiple issues of conflict, which tend to get bogged down in the courts. Thus, the logic of the juridical field in complex societies turns our attention to identifying techniques of conflict resolution that are best suited to the conflict at hand so that, to paraphrase Dezalay (1994), 'the forum' will fit 'the fuss'.

This shift from mediation as a situated community practice to a conflict resolution technique is also a result of the second key factor in the history of mediation: the role of capitalism. The capitalist system, with its ideology of competition and individualism, contributed to the pluralism that was part of the downfall of community-based mediation. The emerging merchant class also contributed to the transformation of mediation into an alternative legal technique. After initially enlisting the Crown's support for the legal regulation of commercial activities, this group soon found the formal law overbearing and too rigid in many respects. In contrast, it saw negotiated dispute resolution practices as more suitable to its economic interests and so embraced mediation. Business conflicts dealt with by the formal legal system could be costly and publicly embarrassing, whereas facilitators familiar with the needs and interests of business could offer private and confidential mediated or arbitrated justice (Auerbach, 1983; Dezalay, 1994). For example, in the late-nineteenth century, American capitalists advocated mediation and informal arbitration as better ways by which to expedite negotiation among business disputants, who were seen as members of an 'industrial family' united by shared interests (Auerbach, 1983, p 64). Despite state-centred efforts to achieve legal domination for the juridical realm, the business domain strove to preserve mediation as a dispute resolution practice.

As Western societies entered the twentieth century, the informal–formal justice complex began to define the juridical field. No longer was there a space outside of law and the state for the undisturbed practice of informal justice; instead, mediation was inserted firmly within the juridical field, co-existing with formal justice practices by dutifully playing the role of a secondary justice option within a developing legal market. It would thus be left to a new set of activists to rediscover mediation as a community practice and to attempt to break free of the informal–formal justice complex.

The community mediation movement

Community mediation arose in North America in the 1970s as a response to dissatisfaction with the formal administration of justice (see Augusti-Panareda, 2005; Harrington, 1985; Hedeen and Coy, 2000; Merry and Milner, 1995; Pavlich, 1996a). It was argued that the institutional rigidity, adversarialism and coerciveness of a court system monopolised by justice professionals, and conducted in the erudite language of law, led to a justice experience that was alienating and disempowering. As an alternative, advocates of community mediation proposed the 'community' as a normative space in which conciliatory and participatory forms of justice could be enacted.

These views were bolstered by a cultural context in which the Civil Rights Movement and the identity politics of the New Left had inspired an individual and collective empowerment sensibility among activists (Coy and Hedeen, 2005). Social movement energies turned away from a singular focus on matters of economic redistribution and instead prioritised matters of cultural recognition, in the form of demands for acknowledgement of previously ignored or despised identities (Fraser, 1997). With this new thrust came an increased emphasis on group autonomy and the 'community' was a common rallying point for these sentiments.

In addition, the decline of the welfare state, because of its alleged inefficiencies, alongside heightened scepticism of 'big government', sparked an attitude that state steering was no longer a prerequisite for achieving social justice. More and more, new polities of local control were conceived and, among these, the 'community' loomed large as an organisational structure viewed as worthy of rediscovery. Thus, state involvement in community life came to be seen with greater suspicion, as activists sensed the threat of state control lurking within all forms of state intervention.

Community justice centres, community credit unions, neighbourhood-based health and food co-operatives, and other local experiments were established under this new logic (Coy and Hedeen, 2005). In the case of community justice centres, lay mediators volunteered to facilitate the resolution of neighbourhood-based disputes. Initially, it was expected that these mediators would attend to both civil and minor criminal cases; over time, however, they came to focus primarily on civil disputes (Olson and Dzur, 2004).

The effectiveness of lay mediators was said to rest in their powers of moral suasion and community status, not in their position or formal training. More importantly, these lay mediators were to be people who would not be inclined to seek personal power through their positions; instead, they would selflessly assist in the spread of community-based peace and democracy. For example, the San Francisco Community Boards (SFCB), thought to be one of the most dedicated examples of community justice at the time (Fitzpatrick, 1995), sought to build community harmony by addressing conflicts before they exploded in violent and divisive struggles, by reducing fear of crime within the community and by empowering residents with dispute resolution skills that they could apply in their daily lives (Shonholtz, 1984). During SFCB encounters, disputants would present their conflict to members of a volunteer-based panel, which would attempt to facilitate a consensual and conciliatory resolution. The members of this panel would be selected based on characteristics shared with the disputants rather than on perceptions of social status or power. Presumably, these shared characteristics would allow the disputants to feel more comfortable with, and better understood by, the panel. It also helped to establish a sense of equality among all participants in the SFCB process, so that the disputants would trust their own authority within the process rather than look to panel members for decisive interventions.

Justice experiments such as this one were established throughout North America and Europe. The dedication of their advocates inspired a certain amount of hope for these processes, but it was not long before concerns were raised in respect of the achievements of community mediation and its underlying goals.

Co-optation and professionalisation

Soon after the emergence of community mediation, critics began to question its idealism. In particular, state control critics (see Chapter 1) were concerned that community mediation would be co-opted in the service of state power. Rather than empowering communities and community members, community mediation was viewed as a subtle means of extending state ideologies into communities and enrolling volunteer mediators in the task of governing community behaviour (Abel, 1982; Hofrichter, 1982; Matthews, 1988). For some, this strategy corresponded to the shifting nature of the capitalist state, whereby new regulatory responses were required to deal with the state's fiscal and legitimacy crises after the dismantling of the welfare state (see, for example, Abel, 1982; Selva and Böhm, 1987). For others, community mediation was a ruse (Abel, 1982)—a new tool of capitalist hegemony serving to maintain worker passivity in the face of capitalist crisis (Hofrichter, 1987) and helping to domesticate a potentially rebellious workforce.

In sum, state control critics highlighted that mediation was not an 'alternative', as it presented itself. Under close scrutiny, community mediation programmes proved to be closely tied to bureaucratic systems and the logic of formal justice (Harrington, 1985; Tomasic, 1982). State actors provided referrals to these programmes, funding relationships were formed with various levels of government, and state-defined practice standards and objectives quickly made their way into community mediation. Moreover, legalistic reasoning continued to hold sway over both community mediation practitioners and participants. Such reasoning is predominant in Western societies, because the pervasiveness of the juridical field has inculcated the ethos of law into every person's daily life (Ewick and Silbey, 1998). Consequently, the norms of the juridical field often serve as the basis for much of an individual's private reasoning in relation to disputes. For all of these reasons, it was held that community mediation had failed to return to the small-scale ideal of community-controlled justice.

Subsequent to the above criticisms, others further argued that mediation, and alternative dispute resolution more generally, followed an 'order maintenance' rather than 'law enforcement' strategy of governance (Harrington, 1985). In other words, community mediation was perceived to be embedded within an overarching ideology of legalism and governance, and therefore could not be accorded status as an 'alternative' to these social forces. While proponents of this approach did not see the state orchestrating informal justice in every aspect of its operation, the interests of government were viewed as nonetheless at work within informal justice, in that informal justice practices assisted in the reproduction of the dominant social order. In this sense, this perspective represents an important bridge between the state control critique of community justice and the emerging governmentality studies position that we will discuss later in this chapter. Through these critics, more emphasis came to be placed on governance through the diffusion, rather than concentration, of power, as power seeped into community life through the efforts of various actors, ranging from therapists to spiritual and community leaders.

The external pressures inducing the corruption and co-optation of mediation described by the state control critics were coupled with internal pressures toward market formation, consolidation and professionalisation. In the immediate aftermath of the founding of the community mediation movement, the legal community paid mediation little notice, although some certainly saw it as a threat to legal professionals' monopoly on justice. Among these legal professionals, mediators were cast as untrained, irresponsible and potentially dangerous usurpers of the juridical field. But this oppositional stance toward mediation soon transformed into a desire to appropriate mediation for the lawyer's toolkit. Part of the rationale behind this appropriation was a perception that the legal system was in crisis and would be overrun with cases if it did not implement efficiencies. In the USA, the 1976 Pound Conference on the Causes of Popular Dissatisfaction with the Administration of Justice struck the alarm bell and, through it, Supreme Court Justice Warren Burger spoke to the coming crisis of legal legitimacy. In his view, law needed to diversify its practices or face growing public dissatisfaction (Burger, 1979). This same discovery came later in the UK, sparked by Lord Woolf's 1995–96 inquiry into access to justice in the English courts. In his final report, Lord Woolf recommended a reformed civil justice system that made every effort to avoid litigation, which resulted in the 1999 Code of Procedural Rules that obliged courts to encourage disputants to use alternatives to litigation such as mediation (Nesic, 2001).

It is therefore in the last thirty years that Western legal professionals and state officials have become intensely interested in mediation as a cost-effective and time-efficient alternative to the courts. Neither group, however, has been able to envision justice fully outside of the formal legal system, as idealised by the community mediation movement. Instead, they have developed state-sanctioned and state-mandated forms of mediation to compete with the community mediation vision. One prominent example of the latter is the so-called 'Michigan Mediation' model, which was established in 1983 by the Federal District Court for the Western District of Michigan. According to Rule 42 of this process, as an alternative to the courts 'a panel of three attorney-neutrals consider 30-min presentations from each party and return an evaluation of the case' (Coy and Hedeen, 2005, p 414; see also Plapinger and Stienstra, 1996). Similar state-sanctioned mediation processes have been implemented in other jurisdictions. In Canada's British Columbia (BC), Notice to Mediate legislation was enacted in April 1998 to decrease pressures on the courts. This legislation enables any party in certain cases (for example, small claims, construction and personal injury) to compel the other(s) to participate in mediation. This requires only that the other party take part in mediation—not that the case is settled within this forum. With the implementation of the Notice to Mediate, the BC Attorney General's Dispute Resolution Office urged interested parties to select mediators from the BC Mediator Roster, which 'can provide access to trained and experienced mediators who have agreed to abide by an established code of conduct' (Homeowner Protection Office, 1999). Thus, the government authorised a group of 'professional' mediators to mediate specific types of disputes.

Even mild forms of state accreditation such as these, not to mention the access to cases and the regular livelihood they provide, come with market- and state-defined expectations. For instance, the mandatory mediation of small claims construction cases in some court registries in British Columbia is accompanied by expectations of an 85 per cent satisfaction rate and a 60 per cent settlement rate for mediators, all while operating within the confines of a single, two-hour mediation session for each case. The rules of small claims mediation in British Columbia, unlike those of 'Michigan Mediation', strictly forbid mediators from providing disputants with legal advice; nonetheless, mediators in this context will likely feel the need to be more assertive in settling disputes in order to meet expectations and maintain access to a court-sponsored caseload.[1]

Moreover, as governments and businesses slowly embrace mediation, its practice has become more financially rewarding, with some mediators charging upwards of $200 per hour. This is not, however, to suggest that there is ample work for mediators, because an explosion of mediator training programmes has saturated the market (Woolford and Ratner, 2005) and the take-up of mediation has been modest in many jurisdictions (for example, the UK; see Nesic, 2001; Glaister, 2001). In several regions, we see that there are numerous mediators competing for limited, but profitable, cases, which has resulted in a situation in which certain actors within the mediation field have sought to professionalise mediation, so as to hinder competition and secure a lucrative clientele. This includes efforts to establish mediation certification through training programmes, to formulate codes of ethics for the regulation of mediation practice and to form professional associations that mobilise to increase mediators' share of the juridical market (see Morris and Pirie, 1994). Ostensibly, these developments are directed toward preventing unqualified and untrained individuals from unwarrantedly claiming to be mediators; they also perform a vital market function, however, by placing limits on who may and who may not access mediation cases within the juridical field.

The fragmentation of mediation

In recent times, with forces of co-optation and professionalisation pulling mediation in different directions, the practice of mediation has fragmented in two key ways. First, mediation sites have multiplied as mediation is applied to a growing number of dispute types, including family, construction, small claims, human rights, business and organisational conflicts. This widening of the mediation field is, in part, a result of the professional struggle over the ownership of mediation discussed in the previous section. Lawyers and judges have appropriated mediation as a component of their legal skills set and have entered into direct competition with lay mediators, often wresting from the latter the more high-paying clientele. As well, state gatekeepers have instituted mediator qualifications and training in some jurisdictions. These factors, in addition to increased competition among the surplus of trained lawyer and non-lawyer mediators, have stimulated a diversification of mediation practices. For example, mediators have developed expertise in novel

---

1 Our discussion of mediation in British Columbia is based upon research and interviews conducted between 1999 and 2002 through our participation in a Social Sciences and Humanities Research Council (SSHRC) Community University Research Alliance (CURA) project on alternative dispute resolution in the Faculty of Law at the University of British Columbia.

service products such as 'conflict coaching' that are marketed around the corporate world. According to Noble (2002):

> Conflict coaching is a specialised niche and a dispute resolution technique that unites the fundamentals of coaching and conflict management. The object of this process is to help people one-on-one, to develop and improve the way they deal with workplace conflict.

In general, new mediators are encouraged to seek out 'uncharted' territories in which to offer their services (Seamone, 2000), resulting in the spread of mediation to multiple settings, including schoolyards, sports arenas and workplaces.

Second, the philosophical underpinnings of mediation have fragmented as mediation has moved from being a culturally contextualised community practice to a legal technique. This has resulted in greater differentiation between mediator 'styles'. There is no consensus on the variety of styles of mediation extant within the juridical field. For example, in her review of the mediation literature, Carrie Menkel-Meadow (1995) identifies nine mediation styles: 'facilitative'; 'evaluative'; 'transformative'; 'bureaucratic'; 'open'; 'closed'; 'community'; 'activist'; 'pragmatic'. No system of categorisation is perfect in its application to mediation, because mediators themselves often play different roles and make different interventions depending on the nature of the conflict they face. Nonetheless, most mediators express preferences for particular forms of mediation that are based on various motivating justice frames: transformative, facilitative and evaluative.[2]

Transformative mediation is, perhaps, the mediation type that holds most closely to the ideals of the community mediation movement. It refers to dispute resolution practices that are directed toward effecting a fundamental transformation in the communication patterns used by individuals in conflict. Proponents of this perspective often hold that individual-level transformations of this nature can have broader societal effects if individuals come to view their relationships differently and interact in more positive ways on the basis of their mediation experience (Bush and Folger, 1994). In this manner, it holds to one of the key tenets of community mediation: empowerment. Formal justice is thought to narrow conflicts to a limited set of resolution

---

2   The reasoning behind this limitation is twofold. First, in our empirical research on mediation (Woolford and Ratner, 2005; 2007), these appear to be the most common mediation types. Second, it is our contention that other 'types' of mediation are encompassed by these broad categories. For instance, rather than view community mediation as a distinct category, we see community-based mediation strategies as typically employing either a transformative or a facilitative mediation strategy. Similarly, transformative, facilitative and evaluative mediations exhibit varying degrees of pragmatism—with transformative mediations being the least pragmatic and evaluative mediations the most geared toward utilitarian ends.

options, thereby stifling creativity and encouraging disputants to take a 'weak and selfish' stance with respect to the conflict (Bush and Folger, 1994). Transformative mediation, in contrast, looks to provide disputants with the opportunity for personal growth, offering a new conciliatory framework for understanding disputes that can later spread throughout community and society as individuals learn to practise 'compassionate strength' in all of their relationships (Bush and Folger, 1994, p 229). In practice, these are the goals that motivate transformative mediators rather than an emphasis on settlement at any cost. For such mediators, creating a setting that allows for open dialogue and respectful interaction can be as valuable as a clear resolution to the conflict. Transformative mediators also attempt to minimise interventions, encouraging the parties to carry the process forward by telling their stories in an honest and open fashion, rather than through mediator manipulation.

Facilitative mediation, in contrast, focuses more on processual matters, such as dialogical, non-coercive and non-adversarial communication, rather than on the substantive goals of individual or societal transformation. This form of mediation has grown out of the 'interest-based' negotiation model made popular by Fisher and Ury (1991), which encourages disputants to think of their conflicts in terms of flexible 'interests' rather than rigid and unmovable 'positions'. Facilitative mediators often employ various techniques, such as summarising, reframing and private caucusing, all of which serve to orient the disputants toward conciliatory interaction rather than positional wrangling. Along these lines, a facilitative mediator might reframe a position stated by one disputant in order to highlight the more general interests upon which this sentiment is based. For example, if a family divorce mediation were to centre on accusations of an affair, the following statement might be made: 'He has been cheating on me and now wants to run off and leave me in the poorhouse.' Upon hearing this, the facilitative mediator might reframe the statement as follows: 'So, what you are saying is that honesty and trust are very important to you?' In this way, the mediator will emphasise instead neutral concepts to which all parties can agree. Through interjections such as these, which also serve to model correct conciliatory behaviour to the disputants, the mediator helps to establish and maintain the rules of the mediation.

It is believed that facilitative mediation is more efficient and cost-effective than negotiations or court proceedings carried out through the formal justice system, and that these procedures are more likely to result in disputant satisfaction. Given these more immediate and pragmatic objectives, it is fair to suggest that facilitative mediation seeks more to reform and humanise the formal justice system, rather than to transform it. If carried out effectively, the facilitative approach has the potential to demonstrate to disputants that they have a capacity for interest conciliation that provides them with the empathy and flexibility necessary to reach a compromise.

Finally, in evaluative mediation, the concern for processual and/or trans-formative justice is less prominent (or, in some cases, fully bracketed) in def-erence to the practical goal of settlement. An evaluative mediator is likely to provide disputants with a legal opinion on their conflict or to engage in the practice of aggressive 'reality checking' to move intransigent disputants away from 'impractical' goals. In this sense, evaluative mediation is the approach that is most complementary to the formal legal system, because its primary function is to serve as an expedient means for resolving conflict, thus helping to prevent court backlog. It is, one might say, formal law by other means, because the evaluative mediator obeys a juridical logic in guiding the dispu-tants toward a settlement in accordance with court-dispensed standards. Commercial mediation is the example par excellence of evaluative mediation, because parties engaged in this type of mediation typically seek mechanisms whereby they can avoid the posturing and strategic interactions that charac-terise formal legal proceedings, and which add excessive costs to business operations. Additionally, businesses continue to prefer confidential mediation processes as a way of resolving their disputes and keeping corporate matters out of the public spotlight. This said, they usually do not entrust their dis-putes to neutral facilitators who may lack specific knowledge about the source of the conflict. Instead, they rely on mediators who both have expert-ise in the area of concern (for example, construction law) and who can provide information on the potential litigation outcome if the case were to proceed to court.

Evaluative mediation represents the complete immersion of mediation within the formal legal system and the co-option of the technique, because the instrumental rationality of governance and business dictates the mediation process. In this incarnation, the communicative and social justice function of mediation is surrendered to a purely instrumental logic of dispute resolution.

With the differentiation of mediation sites and practice, it becomes increas-ingly difficult to speak of mediation in a singular sense. Moreover, combined with the growing mainstream acceptance and professionalisation of medi-ation, this development makes a unitary analysis of mediation problematic. Mediation is a manifold set of practices directed toward a variety of object-ives. Thus, attempts to hail mediation as an unqualified improvement on formal justice or to reduce it to the machinations of state control do not sufficiently address the complexity of contemporary mediation practice. For this reason, recent scholars have sought to develop more nuanced conceptual frameworks for understanding mediation both as a means of social control and as a means of communicative power. The first group of scholars that we will examine—governmentality critics of mediation—contends that medi-ation plays a disciplinary and formative role in the constitution of non-conflictive subjects, but that this is not a role that emanates directly from state intentions. The second group—scholars borrowing from Habermas' writings on discourse ethics and communicative action—attempts to specify what sort of communicative conditions are necessary to allow mediation truly to empower its participants. We will examine both of these perspectives en route to situating mediation within the informal–formal justice complex.

Mediation within the informal–formal justice complex

The governmentality critique

Rather than take aim at mediation as a whole, Foucault-inspired critics have, for the most part, focused specifically on community mediation. One strand of this critique examines how community mediation has a *disciplinary* effect on individuals, because it locates them in bounded communities and subjects them to a battery of normative and normalising techniques (Fitzpatrick, 1988).[3] Under this conceptualisation, mediation is not understood as a direct, or even indirect, form of state control; it is rather a diffuse mode of power that operates in local contexts and situations through the efforts of professionals and practitioners to mobilise specific juridical rationalities. Such rationalities are disciplinary, in the sense that they train individuals to conduct themselves in conflict situations in a productive and positive manner that increases the likelihood of resolution. As one facilitative mediator once told us, the objective is 'to teach people without them knowing they are being taught'.[4] In this sense, although a mediator may not be acting at the behest of state power, she is still a potential source of disciplinary force in her efforts to teach disputants how better to resolve their problems. The end result of this power may be the same as that projected by state control theorists—peaceable community subjects who are less prone to resistance—but this derives from actors employing ethical-political programmes and rationalities that are not reducible simply to state orchestration.

More recently, critics have examined community mediation as a 'technology of self' (Pavlich, 1996a; 1996b). This marks the true beginning of what we refer to as the governmentality studies' critique of mediation, because these authors place greater emphasis on Foucault's work on governance (1990; 1991), especially as it relates to governance as a mode of operating on oneself. Pavlich (1996a) has also referred to this as 'pastoral power', referencing Foucault's image of the shepherd concerned for the well-being of his flock. A technology of self, then, is a mode of constituting the 'self' or one's

---

3 These critics were referred to as the '*new informalists*' (Matthews, 1988), because they directed attention away from the formal state and examined the microphysics of power in supposed informal contexts. We have avoided use of this terminology, because many of these authors question the formal–informal dualism.

4 This comment was made in an interview conducted with a Vancouver-based mediator in February 2002.

subjectivity. Each of us is involved in an ongoing project of shaping our self-identity and, in so doing, we draw upon specific logics and rationalities that are socially distributed and contextually coherent. That is, we rely on discourses that exist outside of us and which make sense within the terms of our social lives. Thus, this work upon ourselves takes place within a sociocultural context that informs the sorts of self-identities we might choose and the ways in which we might conceptualise them, and these practices or 'technologies' of self tend toward limited forms of identity building. It is here that we see the close connection between the idea of a technology of self and Foucault's notion of governmentality, with the latter term signalling a shift in practices of governance from oppressive and disciplinary controls, toward providing for the well-being of individuals. In addition, this shift introduces a process of investing in the construction of citizen 'mentalities' that are conducive to governance. These 'mentalities' then begin to operate beyond the ambit of state power, reproducing governable subjects without necessitating active government intervention.

Along these lines, governmentality studies scholars contend that state control criticisms of community mediation are too stark in their suggestion of a co-ordinated government policy to co-opt community-based justice practices. By theorising such a rigid modality of control, state control critics tend to overlook the 'self-constitution' of community members. That is, mediation types such as community mediation and transformative mediation do not simply oppress community members through an extension of state control into the community; more importantly, they play a constitutive role in creating new juridical subjectivities who internalise and enact their governance (see Pavlich, 1996a; Van Krieken, 2001). In other words, they fashion a conciliatory space in which these individuals can work upon themselves, engaging in personal transformations that at once make them more governable.

In this way, mediation represents an instance of what Miller and Rose (1992, p 2) refer to as governance 'at a distance' (see also Rose, 1993; 1996). As discussed in Chapter 2, this entails employing devices of governance that permit detachment between the activities of government and activities in localities. Governing at a distance enables the governance of individuals through their own freedom, encouraging them to make decisions conducive to the logic of neoliberal economic rationalism and to construct themselves as responsible economic actors. Thus, according to the governmentality studies' critique of community mediation, mediation represents one such device of governing 'at a distance' in that it disperses the logic of dispute resolution and conciliation throughout communities without necessitating the more forceful involvement of the state. In Pavlich's terms:

> If community mediation provides a panoptic disciplinary gaze over individuals, it also pressures active subjective (ethical) work. If successful, the confessional ethos of community mediation creates nondisputing

self-identities who take with them a life skill: the ability to 'mediate' their own definitions of self within the 'community' to avoid conflicts arising in the future.

(1996b, p 727)

In this sense, by focusing its discussion on state force, the state control critique of community mediation misses the active role played by subjects in the shaping of their identities.

Another apposite governmentality studies' critique of community mediation targets the rigid distinction between informal and formal justice, suggesting instead the interdependence of both justice forms. As Fitzpatrick (1988, pp 190–2) notes, formal and informal justice are 'mutually constitutive', in that they rely upon one another in significant ways. In this regard, community mediation sets itself against the formal justice system by promising to be everything that the latter is not: if the formal justice system is adversarial, then community mediation will be non-adversarial; if the formal justice system is alienating, then community mediation will be empowering. The same can be said for the formal justice system, which has often relied on informal alternatives to ensure its smooth operation. For example, mediation and arbitration play a role in diverting lesser disputes from the legal system, ensuring that the latter is reserved for 'important' or difficult cases. As well, contending with such 'important' cases helps to reinforce the legitimacy and superiority of the formal legal system, because it comes to be viewed as the final arbiter on crucial societal matters (Dezalay, 1994).

Also at issue in the governmentality studies' critique of community mediation is the very notion of 'community'. As Pavlich suggests:

by (implicitly) defining a 'community' as an entity with specific features, community mediation advocates help to produce and sustain a vision of that to which their regulatory mechanisms are directed.

(1996b, p 112)

In other words, community mediation plays a part in imagining a community and, furthermore, in imagining this as a peaceful and non-coercive space. In so doing, community mediation contributes to fixing the boundaries of community life. But this move is not necessarily an empowering one, because a totalising vision of community can prove, and in many cases has proven, as limiting and oppressive for community members as life under the state. Thus, rather than community representing a liberating, co-operative and conciliatory space, it is also a space marked by forced sameness and often unspoken (but occasionally voiced) exclusions of those who are *not* members of the community.

Brigg (2003) has further explored this exclusionary character of community mediation by focusing on the cultural dimensions of mediation. He argues that not only is mediation grounded within the juridical order, it also has as its backdrop a range of Western concepts about conflict and selfhood. Drawing on Foucault's analysis of the confessional, Brigg suggests that mediation, as a confessional space, places culturally founded, performative expectations on participants:

> In the mediation process, the mediator serves as the figure to whom the disputant confesses and as the one who specifies the parameters for confessing . . . There is a pressure on disputants to perform their stories and selves in ways understandable to the mediators and intelligible within the goals of the mediation session and accompanying assumptions about peace and conflict.
>
> (2003, p 295)

For Brigg, the self that is to be portrayed according to the strictures of the mediation process is a Western self, possessed with a coherent reason and an orientation toward social harmony.

It is likely that much of the governmentality studies' critique of mediation has been focused on the contradictions of community mediation because it is this mediation site that has traditionally made the loftiest promises in terms of offering an alternative, empowering and non-coercive mode of justice. This narrow focus, however, results in governmentality studies offering only a partial understanding of the informal–formal justice complex, because it does not fully capture the volatile and fragmented nature of mediation within civil law. As a result, although this perspective offers a useful insight into how power infiltrates community mediation, it does not provide a picture of the broader patterns of power that operate within the juridical field and the informal–formal justice complex, such as the corruptive influence that mainstream forms of facilitative and evaluative mediation might have on community mediation practices that are intended to be transformative. But before we turn our attention to the multiple levels of power that threaten transformative mediation, we must first explore the ways in which Habermasian theory has been enlisted to guide and strengthen mediation theory and practice.

Communicative action and mediation

Some proponents of mediation have found potential for reconceptualising mediation in the work of Jürgen Habermas, alongside new hopes for preventing the colonisation and juridification of mediation. Chilton and Cuzzo (2005), for example, draw on Habermas' *Theory of Communicative Action*, viewing it as an apt theoretical framework for mediation. They focus primarily on Habermas' conditions for communication, employing them as an anchor for facilitating mediation sessions, paying less attention to the broader social and political conditions that are essential to the ideal speech situation or to mediation's potential to serve as a type of informal public sphere. Under their approach, mediators become referees enforcing the rules of discourse ethics:

> The assumption is that the difficulty in solving a conflict and in repairing a relationship comes from some violation of these presuppositions. The process of mediation then becomes, for mediators personally, a commitment to ensure that these presuppositions are established, fulfilled, and pursued. Knowing these presuppositions can give the mediator a practical checklist of potential areas of breakdown in the process, thereby allowing him or her to suggest opportunities or different directions.
>
> (Chilton and Cuzzo, 2005, pp 327–8)

Indeed, Chilton and Cuzzo attempt to provide examples and guidelines that serve as such a 'checklist'. First, they develop a script for mediators to introduce the presuppositions of discourse ethics once they begin a mediation session. This includes statements such as, 'I assume that both of you are going to be trying to be consistent in your words and actions in this room' and 'When you speak, you should do your very best to say only things that you really believe' (2005, p 334). Second, they provide mediators with a list of possible interventions to use when communicative presuppositions are at stake. For example, if the principle of non-contradiction is violated, a mediator might ask 'That comment seemed inconsistent with your earlier comment about X. Earlier you said Y. Would you mind explaining this a bit more?' (2005, p 335). Or, if the mediator fears that coercion is present within the mediation, they might query 'Does anyone feel afraid or unsafe to express a view? Why?' (2005, p 335).

Thus, Chilton and Cuzzo seek to illustrate the practical application of Habermas' communicative approach to mediation sessions. In so doing, they demonstrate that a mediator who is informed by the theory of communicative action gains valuable insight into conflict, as well as new tools for dealing with distorted or inequitable communication. But because they generally limit their discussion to the role to be played by communicative presuppositions within mediation sessions, Chilton and Cuzzo give insufficient attention to the broader social conditions that are central to the ideal speech situation and the public dimensions of informal justice. In particular, attention must be given to unequal and power-laden social relations that threaten to infiltrate deliberative contexts and undermine communicative interactions. Without a more sophisticated understanding of the potential for external social pressures to impact mediated negotiations, Chilton and Cuzzo's perspective appears unlikely to be able to avoid the colonisation or juridification of mediation sessions.

Augusti-Panareda (2005) takes a broader approach to applying the work of Habermas to mediation. He notes that Habermas locates the practices of informal dispute resolution within the lifeworld and views these practices as a form of resistance against colonisation. Because Habermas does not elaborate further on the role of informal justice, however, Augusti-Panareda seeks to examine the parallels between Habermas' theory of communicative action and community mediation. He suggests that community mediation programmes, such as the San Francisco Community Boards (SFCB), share significant traits with Habermas' ideal speech situation. These include the SFCB emphasis on achieving a consensual resolution to the dispute, the participatory involvement and decision-making power of the disputants, the attempt to facilitate open communication and its efforts to discourage instrumental or strategic forms of communication (Augusti-Panareda, 2005).

One problem that arises in Augusti-Panareda's comparison, however, is that he assesses the ideal of community mediation, as described by SFCB proponents, against the ideal speech situation, when this latter tool is intended for evaluating the communicative capacity of actual interactive settings. Contrasting ideal to ideal is overly abstract and does not provide insight into how communication might be improved in actual discursive contexts, such as by observing SFCB panels in operation and evaluating their communicative potential. Nevertheless, Augusti-Panareda makes a valuable contribution by drawing attention to the threat of colonisation and how external instrumental pressures might corrupt the communicative goals of community mediation. Most importantly, he treats the state control and governmentality criticisms of community mediation not as absolutes that signal the poverty of informal justice, but rather as useful political insights to employ in creating improved forms of community justice.

> Community mediation should see the trends pointed out by the critics as potential dangers and domination threats in the practice of mediation that have to be made explicit in order to be superceded. Moreover, Foucault's work can help us here to detect disempowering trends, such as the conversion of community mediation into a field of expert knowledge handled only by professional interveners (Van Krieken, 2001). Awareness of all these possible autonomy-restricting elements is the first step toward overcoming them.
>
> (Augusti-Panareda, 2005, p 283)

Augusti-Panareda stops short, however, in his use of the Foucaultian perspective to examine critically both community mediation and Habermas' theory of communicative action. He does not fully interrogate the terminology on which he builds his perspective, too often taking terms such as 'community' for granted rather than viewing them as already complicit in a certain vision of social order. Without a deeper investigation of the presuppositions of mediation, it will be difficult to get beyond the restrictions (that is, to penetrate the 'microphysics') of the informal–formal justice complex.

The prospects for mediation in the informal–formal justice complex

Based on the above review, we can begin to situate mediation within the informal–formal justice complex. From the governmentality studies' perspective, we take a message of the importance of understanding the multiple modalities of power affecting the communicative potential of mediation. From communicative action, we draw the lesson that pragmatic discursive settings might be established to maximise this communicative potential. Thus, the task becomes one of understanding complex configurations of power so as to better disrupt them and to mobilise effectively the communicative capacities of individuals in mediated settings.

The quest to combine the seemingly contradictory insights of Foucault and Habermas is, however, made difficult by the multiple and competing forms of mediation operating within the juridical field that defy any singular critique or reconstruction of mediation practice. In some instances, the state control critique of mediation is not entirely unfounded, because mediation does appear to contribute to a widening net of state control, such as in state-mandated and evaluative mediation models designed to pressure disputants to resolve their conflict before they expend much in the way of court resources. In others, mediation appears to be performing a more distinct governmentalising role, such as when facilitative mediators intervene to encourage and teach citizens to be self-reliant in conflict resolution. Yet other forms of mediation, such as transformative mediation, more clearly subscribe to an ethic that resembles a Habermasian communicative ideal, in which the flow of open and honest communication fosters the construction of new political understandings—but even these settings are not entirely free from the technologies of self described by governmentality scholars, because they effectively create a space for participants to perform ethical work upon themselves. In sum, while no mediation type is free from the operation of power, power manifests itself differently across the mediation spectrum and each mediation style presents its own political opportunities and obstacles. Thus, the issue of power demands greater attention.

We understand the configuration of power in which these multiple forms of mediation operate (and which challenges the capacity of mediation to encourage communicative action) to be comprised of three levels:

- broader systems of power;
- power relations within the juridical field;
- power relations within the subfield of mediation.

First, in terms of the broader context of power, Bourdieu (1987) notes that the juridical field is a 'relatively autonomous' domain of social action. This means that, while this field contains practices insulated from structures of power, it nonetheless influences, and is influenced by, external factors. Thus it is expected that modalities and rationalities of power and control will enter into juridical relations from other fields of social activity, such as politics and economics, and that intersections of power across all of these fields of action will create a broader field of power that reproduces dominant social relations. In this sense, power (as understood by Foucault), although diffused throughout the social world, also becomes condensed and invested in certain class positions—positions that Bourdieu defines not by virtue of one's location within the relations of production, but rather in respect of the shared system of dispositions, or 'habitus' (Bourdieu, 1981; 1990)—at specific historical moments.

Under these conditions, it is possible to highlight dominant logics of power that traverse multiple fields of social activity. In the case of the informal–formal justice conflict, we have so far emphasised how neoliberalism has come to play this role. No single field of social activity produces neoliberalism, understood here as a regulatory framework that adapts to local conditions in order to spread rationalities conducive to a globalising capital (for example, flexibilisation, responsibilisation and deregulation). Instead, neoliberalism crosses all of these fields, borrowing techniques of domination from one area of social space and applying them to others. Within the juridical field, and more particularly in the informal–formal justice complex, the logic of neoliberalism has operated through local demands for community-based justice in an attempt to establish or enrol community justice strategies for the purpose of governing populations 'at a distance'. Through such efforts, the hegemony, or common sense character, of neoliberal thinking has seeped into practices of community justice, making them potent sites for governmentalisation.

Second, power relations within the juridical field present challenges for the prospects of communicative mediation practices. The juridical field has long been the site of professional competition and lawyers, as the primary players within this field of power, are the key competitors. They hold a stake in the maintenance of the juridical status quo, because this helps to preserve their monopoly over the practice of dispute resolution, but they also possess an interest in diversifying and expanding their dispute resolution skills to differentiate themselves from their competitors—both other lawyers and purveyors of 'alternative practices'. It is unsurprising, therefore, that—after a brief resistance to, and dismissal of, the practice of mediation—lawyers would eventually attempt to usurp and expand this practice under their own aegis. A consequence of the legal embrace of mediation is, however, that mediation becomes further embedded in the informal–formal justice complex and becomes increasingly unable to separate itself fully from the dominant adversarial logics of the juridical field.

It is not only through the intentions of lawyers, however, that the juridical field comes to blunt the communicative potential of mediation. The diffusion of legal logic occurs over and beyond the aspirations of lawyers. Indeed, legal thinking has become culturally pervasive in our society, because it is a dominant motif in our films, books, television and everyday lives. Moreover, legal reasoning has become common sense in many Western societies, and juridical tropes are applied to many aspects of our lives. Thus, upon entering mediation, or even upon becoming mediators, it is unlikely that individuals are able simply to bracket this juridical reasoning and embrace new pathways of communication.

Given that mediation is embedded in the informal–formal justice complex, with its overarching juridical rationality, it is probable that it will serve to reproduce and revalorise the juridical field. This might occur in two ways. First, by siphoning off cases from the formal legal system and dealing with them through informal methods, mediation may help to obscure some of the inefficiencies and contradictions of this formal system. People who pass through mediation and feel grateful that they have avoided the alienating experience of the courtroom may not interpret their positive reaction to mediation as a critique of formal justice; more likely, they will view the mediation 'alternative' as a component of this formal system, restoring their faith in this system. In this manner, mediation might serve to mitigate rather than to encourage criticism of the formal justice system. Second, because mediation is often applied to cases that are deemed to be 'less serious', this preserves the courtroom for those cases that are perceived to be 'more serious'. As Dezalay (1994) suggests, this division of labour offers the courts a 'profit of distinction', because they are designated the final arbiter for society's most important conflicts. In addition, the formal legal system also profits from the removal of less justiciable cases that might expose the arbitrariness of the courts.

The third threat to the communicability of mediation comes from within the mediation movement itself. As mediation has evolved into a more formalised and socially accepted practice, a mediation market has arisen. As noted earlier in this chapter, this is a potentially lucrative market that is also subject to a great deal of competition, given the growing ranks of professionals marketing themselves as 'mediators'. With these conditions in place, actors try to corner portions of this market through professionalisation and credentialing strategies. Mandatory mediation programmes in some jurisdictions have contributed to this development, because they typically limit the allocation of court-mandated mediation cases to those who meet established qualification standards and code of ethics requirements. With these tendencies toward market competition and professionalisation comes a drift toward instrumental goals and evaluative mediation practices, because mediators begin to direct their efforts toward meeting the prevailing efficiency demands of the market. That is, whether responding to the needs of a mandatory mediation programme or those of their business clientele, mediators are likely to feel the pressures of increased expectations of settlement, as well as those of time and cost savings. To meet expectations, mediators often become more directive in their mediating styles. Transformative mediators may resist these pressures, but they will face the problem of finding sufficient clientele to sustain a viable practice in the already marginalised juridical subfield of mediation.

These three levels of power both overlap and expand on the governmentality studies' critique of informal justice. In them, we can see the governmentalising pressures that disperse rationalities of governance through seemingly local practices such as mediation. But we also see how the internal performative dimensions and market structures of mediation practice lend themselves to a dilution of the communicative goals of some forms of mediation practice.

This does not, however, mean that all communicative potential is bled from mediation. To illustrate this point, we turn our attention to mediation practices themselves to understand how they might allow for empowering moments to arise for mediation clients, providing them with a disruptive or counter-hegemonic perspective on modes of social domination. Nonetheless, under current social conditions, we must also acknowledge that these empowering moments can be difficult to sustain in the aftermath of the mediated session, due to the sorts of social pressures described above.

In terms of the possibility for empowering moments to arise within mediation settings, much depends on the notion of 'empowerment'. Most forms of mediation, like other forms of informal justice, emphasise the empowerment of actors embroiled in conflict in order that they might learn to solve their own problems. If mediation is, as some state control critics suggest, an ideological ruse for furthering state power, then the empowerment felt by individuals through mediation would equate with 'false consciousness', because these individuals would have been duped into thinking that they possess decision-making power. Such a 'strong' state control critique is, however, too blunt. The presence of state control does not necessarily render participants passive and subject to a state-induced false consciousness; indeed, given that participants enter mediation with a variety of expectations and experience it in multiple ways, it is quite possible that one might receive a sense of empowerment even if state control is at work.

For example, in a family mediation established to provide a couple with a conciliatory divorce, several structural factors may be in play, including patriarchal patterns of gender domination, economic power and differentials of social status. The settlement of this dispute might also be quite complementary to state control and basic governance goals; that is, by helping this family to resolve its problems amicably, the state (or social order, if one is sceptical of the notion of 'state') will benefit from its continued existence as a non-disputing, self-regulating family unit. Simply put, bitter divorces can result in lost worker productivity and the interrupted socialisation of children, so there is a governmental interest in reducing the trauma and strife of the divorce process. In addition, a conciliatory divorce can help to reaffirm the importance of the patriarchal family as an economic and child-rearing institution by having couples uphold these values through an amicable divorce, even while they are exiting this form of family life.

Even if we accept this categorically functionalist reading of family mediation, we still cannot discount the possibility of individual empowerment under its terms. If, for instance, the female partner to the marriage, despite her complicity in reaffirming the logic of the patriarchal family, uses family mediation as an opportunity to speak her mind about her husband's controlling behaviour and unfair expectations during their marriage, this may spark in her a new perspective on family and gender domination, offering her new life choices. This is, perhaps, a more minor and uncertain positive result than that which is promised in many texts on mediation and alternative dispute resolution, but its possibility is not unimportant or trifling. It represents an important life event, in the sense that participation in a communicative setting unhinges this individual's patterns of thinking and allows her new insight into the social world. Through this event, she may begin to challenge other patriarchal assumptions and structural inequities that she faces in her everyday life.

But if the communicative standards within the mediation game begin to shift toward evaluative and adversarial standards, as discussed above, the potential for empowerment will be limited to self-serving and instrumental strivings, rather than the more democratic forms of empowerment typically described by mediation advocates. For this reason, evaluative drift remains a serious problem that must be addressed by the mediation movement if mediators want to maintain any semblance of a social justice orientation and to preserve the possibility of genuinely communicative exchanges arising within mediations.

The notion of empowering moments arising within mediation sessions raises a crucial question: are these communicative experiences sustainable after the mediation session has finished, or are the potential benefits of empowerment, conciliation and acknowledgement likely to be fleeting? Returning to our family mediation case, the newly empowered woman who has begun on a path of rethinking the world around her may find that she is subject to numerous social pressures that drive her back toward her disempowered way of being. Her husband's failure to make alimony payments, her lack of job prospects and the increasing needs of her children may lead her to think that she once again needs to find a husband. Moreover, the difficulties associated with dating while caring for children and the demographic fact that there are fewer men available to partner women as they age may lead her, if she is not ready to break with her sexual identity, toward lowered expectations. While this example may be built upon a clichéd and overly traditional heterosexual relationship, we hope it illustrates our point: an eventful moment that provides a person with a new insight on life is not sufficient if social conditions subsequent to this event make it extremely difficult for the individual to act on this insight. To ensure that empowering moments are not mere glimpses of an alternative justice horizon, they must be backed by a communicative power that moves these empowering moments from the informal public sphere and into institutional venues that have legislative powers.

All forms of mediation face the pressures emanating from the levels of power described in this section. This means that the mediation movement must either succumb to the totalising tendencies of the informal–formal justice complex or devise new ways to combat its conditions, and to sustain and expand these empowering moments so that they achieve broader political outcomes. Thus, the question remains as to how this communicative ideal can best be advanced and broadened under the pressures of the informal–formal justice complex and neoliberalism. We will address this important issue in Chapter 6, but before we do so, we must first examine two other forms of informal justice: restorative justice and reparations.

Conclusion

To summarise, in this chapter, we have:

- described the uneven and contradictory development of mediation, as it transformed from a situated community-based practice into an alternative conflict resolution technique within the informal–formal justice complex;
- examined the attempt made by the community justice movement to recapture the communal spirit of traditional mediation, and the subsequent pressures of co-optation and professionalisation that assailed this movement;
- drawn upon the governmentality studies' critique of community mediation to indicate how techniques of discipline and technologies of self operate within mediation sessions;
- highlighted key attempts to employ insights from discourse ethics and the theory of communicative action to improve the practice of mediation, and to guide the mediation movement in protecting itself from system colonisation;
- initiated a reconceptualisation of mediation as a practice embedded within the informal–formal justice complex and subject to various levels of social power. The purpose of this exercise was to highlight the many obstacles facing mediation that prevent it from serving as a

communicative space of citizen empowerment. This analysis will inform our discussion in Chapter 6 in respect of our vision of a political strategy for a reinvigorated, transformative informal justice.

Chapter 4

Restorative justice in the informal–formal justice complex

In this chapter, we discuss competing definitions of restorative justice, examine the origins and development of this justice movement, and identify some of the obstacles and challenges facing restorative justice. This overview sets the stage for an appraisal of the specific place of restorative justice within the informal–formal justice complex, during which we seek to highlight the social and political conditions that need to be addressed in order to realise the communicative potential of restorative justice.

'Restorative justice' is a term that refers to a loose assemblage of criminal justice processes, goals, values, spiritual beliefs, social justice commitments and even lifestyle choices (Johnstone, 2003; see also Strang and Braithwaite, 2001). Restorative justice *processes* typically emphasise the participative involvement of victim and offender, and sometimes the community, in a facilitated encounter. The *goals* of restorative justice include promoting empathy, repairing harm and reintegrating offenders. The *values* of restorative justice centre on key oppositions between restorative and retributive justice. Restorative justice is said to possess values of healing, non-coercion, love, caring and democratic participation that are contrary to the adversarial orientation of formal criminal law, which, according to restorative justice advocates, is punitive, coercive and alienating. Restorative justice has also been represented as consistent with the *spiritual beliefs* of Christians, Jews, aboriginal peoples, Muslims and other religious groups. Likewise, restorative justice is often understood to fit within a broader *social justice* perspective that seeks to transform unjust social relations. Finally, some consider restorative justice a *lifestyle*, in the sense that practitioners and advocates must 'walk the talk' of restorative justice in all dimensions of their everyday lives.

All of these understandings of restorative justice intertwine, making it difficult to define restorative justice in any singular or simple fashion. Nonetheless, efforts have been made to fashion a basic definition. Tony F Marshall (2003, p 28), for example, suggests that 'Restorative Justice is a problem-solving approach to crime which involves the parties themselves, and the community generally, in an active relationship with statutory agencies'. In this manner, he foregrounds the processual qualities of restorative justice.

In contrast, Howard Zehr offers a broader definition that identifies key restorative values:

> Restorative justice is a process to involve, to the extent possible, those who have a stake in a specific offence and to collectively identify and address harms, needs, and obligations, in order to heal and put things as right as possible.
>
> (2002, p 37)

While a processual concern for stakeholder involvement is clear in this definition, Zehr also articulates a key restorative value: making things right in the aftermath of crime.

Such varying definitions of restorative justice are the product of a social movement that, since the 1970s, has engaged in the project of negotiating its self-definition. Part of this conceptualisation process has included attempts to differentiate restorative justice from the competing criminal justice philosophy of retribution. Proponents of restorative justice argue that retributive justice excludes victims and communities from the processes of justice, and transforms offenders into the objects of justice, rather than encouraging them to be active participants in rectifying unlawful behaviour. Restorative justice advocates point out that the traditional criminal justice system is slow to deal with crimes, is costly to maintain, alienates the parties involved in the criminal event and rarely deters offenders from future criminal actions or reintegrates them into society (see Braithwaite, 2003). Thus, restorative justice proponents have sought to build their movement in opposition to the formal criminal justice system.

A brief history of restorative justice

Ancient roots?

The oppositional status of restorative justice is said to rest, in part, in its origins as a conflict resolution practice directed toward achieving communal harmony—one that was eventually eclipsed by state-based retributive justice (Zehr, 1990). According to the historical narrative to which many restorative justice advocates adhere, the gradual centralisation and concentration of state power led to the 'theft' of crime and conflict from families and communities (Christie, 1977). In this view, whereas small-scale social units were once able to respond to conflict in an amicable and creative fashion, since the twelfth century the state has sought to place its interests at the forefront of justice practices, claiming for itself the roles of both victim and accuser. This, it is argued, left victims and the communities in which the conflicts occurred without a voice in resolving the harm done to them (Christie, 1977).

Much like advocates of mediation, proponents of restorative justice trace the lineage of their practices back to multiple cultural sites. Indigenous societies, for example, are often viewed as a primary historical source of restorative justice (Johnstone, 2002) with indigenous traditions of bringing together community members to discuss conflicts idealised as a justice strategy worthy of emulation. Indeed, we see today the re-emergence of some indigenous justice practices (for example, Canadian aboriginal healing circles and the Maori family-based justice conferences) as they are borrowed and redeployed in contemporary justice settings (Ross, 1996). In the USA, the Navajo have reinvigorated the practice of peacemaking circles in their communities. According to Navajo tradition, a person who has been harmed is permitted to make a demand that the offending party undertake some form of remedial action. With the help of a respected community leader (or *naat'aanii*) the disputing parties, along with their families and other affected clan members, then meet to discuss the harm. A prayer begins the meeting to focus all participants on the issue at hand and, subsequently, each party details their version of the events that transpired. Everyone present is then given the opportunity to speak about their thoughts and feelings in respect of the conflict and how it should be resolved (Yazzie and Zion, 2003).

There are, however, dangers attached to drawing too strong a connection between indigenous justice traditions and contemporary restorative justice practices. First, as we noted with respect to the historical lineage of mediation, we are comparing and combining justice practices that derive from different historical and societal contexts. As society has become more pluralistic and more complex, we have ceased to share the commonality of belief and social solidarity that once made modes of indigenous justice practicable.

Second, issues arise in respect of the historical process of colonisation and its continuing impact upon indigenous communities. Colonial powers imposed Western legal traditions on many indigenous groups and tried to extinguish their culturally distinct justice practices. Now, because governments are beginning to recognise that indigenous justice traditions might be used to contend with indigenous crimes, indigenous justice is often being refashioned to complement dominant Western legal traditions and to reinforce state sovereignty. Thus, whereas indigenous justice forms were once an integral part of a holistic community lifestyle, they now function within the hierarchical dictates of former colonial states. For example, 'circle sentencing', a practice that involves gathering victim, offender and community members together in a circle to discuss a wrongdoing and how it might be resolved, has become part of the Canadian juridical fabric. This was seen as a necessary corrective to a legal system that Aboriginal Peoples found to be culturally foreign and which resulted in many injustices (see Royal Commission on Aboriginal Peoples, 1996). Circle sentencing is now, however, often applied in a blanket fashion, regardless of whether or not it is consistent with the particular Aboriginal group's historic practices. In addition, while some room is made for introducing culturally appropriate rituals into the circle-sentencing model (for example, opening prayers or sweetgrass burning), they are combined with (and, in some cases, appear secondary to) Euro-Canadian legal practices, exemplified by the presence of a judge, Crown prosecutor and defence attorney within the circles. While these individuals are not accorded a privileged position within the circle, enabling them to monopolise discussion, they do have authoritative input into the sentencing decision. This is especially true of the judge, who must determine whether or not the community-derived sentence is consistent with Canadian legal norms.

Restorative justice advocates also point to various spiritual traditions as sources for restorative justice. Christianity, for instance, particularly in the figure of Jesus Christ and the emphasis placed on practices such as forgiveness and redemption, has been influential in the development of restorative justice (Allard and Northey, 2003; see also Consedine, 1995). Specific Christian sects have long been vocal advocates for restorative justice: Mennonites were at the helm of one of North America's first restorative justice experiments (see below) and Quakers adhere to a pacifist philosophy that is consistent with a restorative justice perspective on non-violence. Similarities have also been noted between some forms of restorative justice encounter and Quaker meetings, in which worshippers sit in a circle with no one member of the meeting privileged to speak any more than is another (Sherman, 2001). It is not only Christianity that exhibits a tradition of restorative thinking, however. Braithwaite (2003, p 89) goes so far as to state: 'I have yet to discover a culture which does not have some deep-seated restorative traditions.' Along these lines, Bishop Desmond Tutu (2000) attributed the restorative justice model implicit in the South African Truth and Reconciliation Commission (see Chapter 5) to the Bantu tradition of Ubuntu—the notion that a person is a person through other people—which stresses collective interdependency and the need for harmonious community relations.

Such claims to ancient spiritual roots do, however, raise concerns among some contemporary critics of restorative justice. Christian societies have often proven to be punitive in their orientation to criminal justice, although some would argue that this is a result of Christians forgetting the restorative foundations of their justice traditions.[1] Other observers contend that a Christian inflection burdens victims with unrealistic expectations of forgiveness and demands selflessness, especially in cases in which these qualities may not meet the healing needs or match the value systems of these victims (Acorn, 2004).

---

1 Some attribute this forgetting to the historical shift that Christianity made from a marginal movement to a dominant state-sponsored religion (Allard and Northey, 2003). The latter status brought Christianity into alignment with the repressive goals of governance.

The restorative justice movement

Despite its ancient lineage, restorative justice truly took hold as a social movement in the 1970s, around the same time that community mediation emerged. One of the earliest restorative justice experiments, the Kitchener Ontario Victim Offender Reconciliation Program (VORP), took place in 1974, after a vandalism spree by two teenagers in nearby Elmira, Ontario, inspired probation officer Mark Yantzi to propose to the judge that the offenders meet with their victims. As a Mennonite, Yantzi was interested in taking a peacemaking approach to criminal justice, but he never expected the judge to agree to his proposal and to assign to him the task of facilitating meetings between the teenagers and their victims. He and David Worth, who worked for the Mennonite Central Committee, took on this challenge, and its encouraging results—the teenagers faced their victims and paid restitution—spurred them to create a post-sentencing restorative justice project dedicated to reconciling offenders with their victims (Peachey, 2003).

Experiments such as this one resonated with citizens and justice professionals looking for a new approach to crime and offenders. Previous efforts to address the persistent social problem of crime, such as rehabilitation, had come under serious criticism. For some, the rehabilitation and diversion programmes of the 1960s and early 1970s, which were intended to decentralise and deprofessionalise criminal justice, were viewed rather as yet another vehicle for increasing state-directed social control (Cohen, 1985), because rehabilitation professionals were dispersed within communities to contend with what often amounted to minor crimes. For others, dissatisfaction stemmed from the requirement of rehabilitation programmes for a huge investment of social resources to achieve very minor, if any, reductions in recidivism (Martinson, 1974). These latter scholars often recommended a shift in criminological focus, from the quest for rehabilitation, toward the goal of crime prevention—a call subsequently taken up by 'administrative' criminologists seeking to manage and reduce the risk of crime rather than to eradicate it (Young, 1999). But not all were willing to succumb to the pessimism of 'nothing works' (Martinson, 1974; see also Duguid, 2000), and some criminal justice theorists and practitioners saw, in programmes such as the Kitchener VORP, a means for imagining a 'healing' justice different from that proposed by the much criticised model of rehabilitation. For them, the issue became more than that of lowering offender recidivism through a medical or psychiatric model of treatment; instead, they took as their primary task the goal of fostering an 'alternative' justice that would allow offender reintegration, victim healing and the building of community harmony.

This justice movement found support among many existing justice communities, including the prisoner rights, restitution, community justice and victim rights movements (Daly and Immarigeon, 1998). It began to take distinct shape, however, through the efforts of several theorists. Nils Christie

(1977), for example, redefined conflict from a regrettable social problem to a valued property. He argued that, by depriving communities of the work of resolving local conflicts, the state 'stole crime' from communities and thereby stunted the growth of their problem-solving capabilities. Other theorists such as Randy Barnett (1977) and Howard Zehr (1995) announced the emergence of a 'paradigm shift' in criminal justice from retributive to restitution-based or 'restorative' justice, outlining how an alternative justice system might correct the punitive and counter-productive tendencies of retribution. In Australia, John Braithwaite (1989) brought forward similar concerns in his theory of 'reintegrative shaming', which called for a positive form of criminal shaming that reconnected offenders to their families and communities, rather than leaving them alienated and isolated from social support. All of these ideas were eventually brought under the aegis of 'restorative justice', giving a common name to an assemblage of criticisms, concepts and theories. Soon, more theorists joined the movement, building a literature that argued for a holistic approach to criminal harm that jointly considered the healing needs of victims, offenders and communities (see Cragg, 1992; Marshall, 1995; Wright, 1991).

Alongside scholarly efforts to define a new paradigm of criminal justice, practitioners experimented with the possibilities of restorative justice. VORPs similar to the Kitchener programme appeared across North America, as well as victim–offender mediation (VOM) programmes that operated on principles similar to those guiding the community mediation movement (see Chapter 3). In New Zealand, state recognition was given to restorative justice practices in the form of the 1989 Children, Young Persons and Their Families Act, which, in part, attempted to respond to concerns about the over-representation of Maori youth in New Zealand correctional institutions. Through this legislation, family group conferences (FGCs) were introduced, bringing together victims and offenders, and their families and supporters, to resolve criminal incidents. Soon thereafter, in the early 1990s, the small Australian city of Wagga Wagga introduced a police cautioning scheme that combined the framework of New Zealand's FGCs with Braithwaite's notion of reintegrative shaming, establishing police-led conferences to deal with young offenders (see Moore and O'Connell, 2003). The Wagga Wagga programme also inspired similar efforts in the mid-1990s by the UK's Thames Valley Police (Pollard, 2000). Finally, sentencing circles were implemented in Canada as state-sanctioned conflict resolution practice in 1992, beginning with the efforts of Judge Barry Stuart and the Yukon Territorial Court, whereby concerned community members were invited to reflect upon and provide potential resolutions for criminal cases (Cayley, 1998).

These early successes of the restorative justice movement have been followed by others, as restorative justice continues to receive national and international recognition in many jurisdictions. In England and Wales, the Youth Justice and Criminal Evidence Act (1999) adopts the language of restorative justice to describe sanctions for young offenders (Crawford and Newburn, 2002), as does the 2003 Canadian Youth Criminal Justice Act (see below). In 2002, the United Nations released its guidelines for applying restorative justice to criminal matters, touting restorative justice as a legitimate and beneficial means for dealing with criminal harms (United Nations Economic and Social Council, 2002; see also the United Nations, 2007).

With growing state, and international, acceptance of restorative justice, however, critics have begun to question whether officialdom will approve a restorative justice that remains faithful to the ideals of grass-roots empowerment and democratic participation espoused by its early advocates. The spectres of state co-optation and professionalisation lend caution to any premature claims of 'success'.

Co-optation and professionalisation

As with community mediation, critics have charged that restorative justice is prone to state co-optation. Along these lines, Levrant et al (1999) have noted that there is a potential for 'net-widening' through restorative justice (see also Van Ness and Heetderks Strong, 1997; Umbreit and Zehr, 1996; Wright, 1991) if restorative programmes are saddled with minor offences that would otherwise most likely be ignored by the criminal justice system (for example, wrongs as trifling as snowball and shoplifting offences). While such offences may have serious consequences—a snowball might lead to a deadly car crash or frequent shoplifting to business closure—it is questionable whether these wrongs need to be dealt with as criminal offences, which, even in the more affirmative environment of restorative justice, could nonetheless bring unnecessary stigmatisation to youthful wrongdoers. Moreover, dealing with such offences extends criminal justice more deeply into everyday life, as problems within families, schools and communities come to be treated by quasi-official facilitators and mediators, rather than by actors located within these settings.[2]

A related criticism is that restorative justice may become little more than an 'add-on' to the machinery of criminal justice (Wright, 1991; Woolford and Ratner, 2003). Under such conditions, restorative justice might compromise its values commitment in order to fit within the conventions of current criminal justice practices. Youth crime, once again, provides telling examples of this threat. Serge Charbonneau (2004) notes that, although Canada's 2003 Youth Criminal Justice Act makes room for the restorative practice of

---

2 Not all restorative justice programmes necessarily import facilitators into community settings. For example, school-based restorative justice programmes often use peer mediators and, more generally, seek to transfer conflict resolution skills to the broader school community (Morrison, 2005). These strategies, however, also imply the spread of governmentality, even in the absence of a direct form of social control.

conferencing, it also authorises punitive responses for violent and repeat young offenders. This dual approach to youth justice results in the knitting together of restorative and retributive sanctions, with conferencing serving as a disciplinary option for minor offences; the court-based resources of the criminal justice system are reserved for offences considered to be more serious. In this manner, restorative justice becomes a diluted, and potentially net-widening, modality of justice, because it is restricted to offences that might otherwise have been ignored by the criminal justice system, were it not for the availability of this less formal (and less expensive) intervention.

Another criticism that might be raised in respect of the potential for restorative justice to be co-opted has to do with the social location of the restorative justice movement. It has been suggested that restorative justice operates in the realm of 'civil society' (Strang and Braithwaite, 2001), an institutional space between the private world of the family and the centralised power of the state. It is not, however, always clear that restorative justice is separate from the state (for example, many of its advocates are employees of the state who work in the criminal justice system). Clearly, the heavy involvement of criminal justice professionals, as well as the fact that the implementation of restorative justice policies has been largely dependent upon state funding and support, makes dubious any claim to autonomy or separation from the formal justice system (Sullivan et al, 1998).

More importantly, to serve effectively as an institution of civil society, one would expect greater involvement from grass-roots members in the construction and direction of the restorative justice movement. In contrast, the people that restorative justice aims to help rarely participate in leading and organising the movement. Instead, they typically become involved after a restorative justice encounter has been initiated, as participants in the restorative meeting. This is, in part, a consequence of restorative justice being under the rubric of 'criminal justice', because it is the criminal event that triggers the restorative justice encounter and therefore determines who is, and who is not, to be involved in specific restorative justice meetings. Although it is certainly true that members of victim support organisations and some prisoner's rights groups have voiced their support for the restorative justice movement (Bazemore and Umbreit, 1995), victims and prisoners are not the primary players in its mobilisation. Instead, this is more typically a role played by middle-class professionals and actors working at various non-governmental organisations (for example, John Howard and Elizabeth Fry Societies, youth centres). With the predominance of these individuals in leadership roles, the restorative justice movement takes on a top-down appearance that contradicts its inclusive and democratic ideals.

Other critics have raised questions about the apolitical stance of restorative justice (Woolford and Ratner, 2003; Pavlich, 2005), which denies the restorative justice movement an adequate framework for assessing the perils of co-optation under certain social, political and economic conditions. Van

Ness and Heetderks Strong (1997, p 156) suggest that '[r]estorative justice is neither a conservative nor a liberal agenda'. Such ambivalence often prevents critical interrogation of the political agendas at play in the state acceptance and institutionalisation of restorative justice. Because '[r]estorative justice as a social movement can embrace both "neo-liberalism", with its focus on economic rationality, entrepreneurial activity, and concern to "empower the consumer", and grass-roots forms of democratic socialism' (Daly and Immarigeon, 1998, p 31), it is adaptable to multiple social contexts and political (mis)uses. Indeed, to date, restorative justice has frequently been embraced by neoliberal nations concerned with fiscal conservatism (Braithwaite, 1996), who have been able to deploy restorative justice in the interest of reducing the machinery of the state without sacrificing a requisite measure of social regulation. If incorporation of restorative justice practices becomes the sole goal of the restorative justice movement, without concern for the political values that underlie this incorporation, then movement members should not be surprised to see an assault on their values as their programmes are shifted to meet the needs of neoliberal governance.

The lack of grass-roots involvement in and the political ambivalence of the restorative justice movement are related to questions regarding the role of professionals within restorative justice. The early advocates of restorative justice, although often themselves 'professionals' of various stripes (for example, academics and probation officers), did not foresee much professional involvement in restorative justice practices (see Christie, 1977). Nevertheless, as Olson and Dzur (2004, p 139) note: 'Restorative justice largely ignores the role of professionals, and yet professionals have played a dominant part in initiating many restorative justice programs.' For example, the John Howard Society of Manitoba co-manages a restorative justice programme called 'Restorative Resolutions' with the provincial Manitoba government in the city of Winnipeg. This programme is highly regarded as one of the most successful in Canada and studies suggest that it has been relatively successful in reducing rates of recidivism (Bonta et al, 1998). It is, however, far from a model of deprofessionalised justice. The Restorative Resolutions office houses between eight and ten caseworkers, who are employees of the provincial government and many of which have past experience as probation officers or in another role within the criminal justice system. When they receive a referral, typically from another professional—a defence or Crown attorney, a police officer, a probation officer or a judge—they will work with the referred offender (and, in some cases, the victim as well) to create a restorative plan as an alternative sentence. This plan will be presented to a judge, who will decide whether the plan represents a reasonable and safe response to the crime committed.

In this instance, and in many others, professionals are involved at every step of the restorative justice process. Moreover, as with mediation, there are moves afoot to provide restorative justice caseworkers with greater degrees of training and to increase entry-level qualifications and credentials. While restorative justice was initially idealised as a project that could be implemented by lay facilitators, it soon became apparent that criminal justice cases frequently involve issues that are cause for great emotional strain between disputants. It is also the case that disputants often possess unequal amounts of power. The wrongdoer, having harmed the victim, may be in a position to intimidate or threaten the victim further, sometimes in the subtlest of ways. At the same time, however, the wrongdoer is also participating in restorative justice in the shadow of the criminal justice system, knowing that the force of this system will weigh down upon him if the restorative encounter is unsuccessful. These and other aspects present the potential for painful, or even traumatic, moments to emerge within the restorative encounter and questions might be raised as to whether or not lay facilitators are likely to be prepared for these challenges. Moreover, because participants in the restorative encounter are expected to arrive at a sanction or healing plan for the wrongdoer, serious problems can arise if they are not fully aware of the types of service available to help the wrongdoer. For instance, it is of little use for the participants in a restorative encounter to recommend anger management if there are no available spaces in local anger management programmes. Thus, a trained facilitator, or other professionals who might join community members as part of a restorative justice meeting, can offer important information to supplement the restorative process (Olson and Dzur, 2004). But is it possible for these professionals to leave aside their training and juridical indoctrination, and to embrace restorative justice principles on their own terms? We will consider this question in greater detail later in the chapter, but before we do so, we must consider some of the programmatic variations within restorative justice.

The fragmentation of restorative justice

A social movement is rarely a uniform and cohesive body. Within the broad scope of a social movement, there are often multiple social movement organisations (see McCarthy and Zald, 1973; 1977; Diani, 1992). There are also actors that compete with one another to 'frame' (Snow and Benford, 1992; Snow et al, 1986)—that is, to identify interpretive schemata for understanding the grievances and goals of the movement—the issues and objectives that guide the movement's activity.

The competition between opposing visions of restorative justice is evident in the restorative justice movement. Elsewhere, we have identified two ideal-typical characterisations of the organisations that operate within the boundaries of this movement (Ratner and Woolford, 2002; see also Woolford and Ratner, 2003).[3] We describe the first set of restorative justice organisations as

---

3 Braithwaite (2002) has developed a similar distinction between *administrative* and *social justice* strands of restorative justice.

'governmentalist'. Governmentalist organisations typically function as local divisions of the criminal justice system, and serve to discipline and 'responsibilise' offenders by using the force of the restorative encounter to spread socially conventional normative expectations. Although ostensibly based on community values, the goals of such programmes are largely consistent with the regulatory interests of the neoliberal state. They seek to encourage individuals to internalise non-disputing behaviours, so that they become self-policing and self-governing actors. Moreover, the low cost of their largely volunteer-run operations appeals to politicians concerned with balancing state budgets. Governmentalist restorative justice programmes respond to this neoliberal desire for cost savings by emphasising the money saved by the criminal justice system when offenders are processed through restorative justice rather than through the courts. In this sense, in contrast to social movements that eschew instrumental thinking, governmentalist restorative justice practitioners are not averse to directing their practices toward achieving managerialist goals and are willing to accept a degree of programmatic definition in exchange for increased state contributions to the maintenance of their operations.

A second category of organisations within the restorative justice movement can be described as 'communitarian'. In opposition to the governmentalists, communitarians view restorative justice as a form of social justice tailored to meet the specific needs of the community in which it is implemented, or for a variety of 'communities of care' or micro-communities (McCold and Wachtel, 1998)—communities based on social relationships and attachments rather than geographic propinquity—that are served by the restorative justice programme. For practitioners who adhere to a communitarian perspective, restorative justice programmes need to maintain a careful distance from the formal criminal justice system in order to allow for community autonomy in the shaping of local justice options. This autonomy is difficult to maintain, however, because the primary sources for referrals for these programmes are the police and the courts. Moreover, the funding required by these programmes, although relatively minimal, typically comes from criminal justice system sources. These factors lead to increased pressure on communitarian restorative justice practitioners to design their justice processes in a manner that is complementary to the formal justice system in order to secure vital referrals and funding.

Communitarian practitioners of restorative justice often resist attempts to dilute the restorative thrust of their programmes by seeking out alternatives to dependence on the criminal justice system. For example, they open their processes to accept referrals from local schools or the community, bypassing the mechanisms of the formal justice system and including in their activities conflicts other than those defined as 'criminal'. They also attempt to diversify their funding sources, looking to local community-based funding opportunities. Finally, they stress the importance of their restorative justice values on the understanding that a firm attachment to their values will prevent them from allowing the co-optation of their programmes. This includes efforts to achieve 'buy-in' for restorative justice values among criminal justice professionals.

Governmentalist and communitarian types of restorative justice also differ in terms of the values, behaviours and habits that they inculcate in their subjects. For governmentalists, the primary concern is to transform offenders into accountable, prosocial, and law-abiding actors, while victim and community participants are encouraged to participate in the future surveillance and disciplinary control of these individuals. In contrast, communitarian restorative justice prioritises the empowerment of all parties so that they come to possess a clear sense of agency over their lives. In the ethical space of communitarian restorative justice, however, these individuals are encouraged to direct their agency toward future peaceful and collaborative interactions. Thus, the emphasis is upon establishing or re-establishing a sense of community among offenders, victims and community members, through which these actors can help and support one another.

Finally, governmentalist and communitarian forms of restorative justice hold contrasting visions of where the movement should situate itself in relation to the informal–formal justice complex. Governmentalist restorative justice practitioners complain about their marginality and seek greater co-operation with the formal justice system, so that their programmes might become an integral component of its operation. In this sense, success for them means the disappearance of the restorative justice movement when restorative justice becomes official state policy. In contrast, communitarians often celebrate their marginal status and view it as a means of greater procedural freedom. With this freedom, they envision restorative justice as an opportunity to construct new community values and social networks—or what they often refer to as 'social capital' (Putnam, 2000)—in a manner that improves the liveability of these communities for all their residents.

There are, however, similarities that cross the governmentalist–communitarian divide. For example, governmentalist programmes often cite a need for offender accountability as a goal of the restorative justice encounter. In the same sense, communitarians often speak of responsibility, if not accountability. Thus, both assume the existence of an individual agent who is the cause of the criminal event, even if they might differ with respect to the extent to which they see other causal factors as having a role in the crime's commission. Both assume that those who suffer as a result of the criminal event are 'victims' who need to be restored, although governmentalist programmes do tend to be more offender-focused. With this assumption comes a sensibility that can be categorised under the philosophy of compensatory justice, in that they both visualise a moral equation whereby a wrongful act must be balanced out in some meaningful manner, with due consideration given to the individual victim's needs. Finally, because they still, for the most part, operate within the framework of 'crime', each is still located within the moral standards defined within codified law. Given these common starting points for both governmentalist and communitarian forms of restorative justice, it is difficult to argue that these are mutually exclusive models of restorative justice. Instead, we suggest that the primary difference between governmentalist and communitarian restorative justice types is a result of their positioning within the informal–formal justice complex, with governmentalist programmes being more firmly lodged within this complex due to the complementarity between their managerialist and responsibilising efforts and those of formal criminal justice.

As in the previous chapter in respect of mediation, we now turn toward the theories of governmentality studies and discourse ethics to help us situate restorative justice in its multiple forms within the informal–formal justice complex.

Restorative justice within the informal–formal justice complex

The governmentality critique

Several scholars have examined restorative justice through a governmentality studies lens (Andersen, 1999; Pavlich, 1999; 2005; Shearing, 2001; Young, 2003). As with mediation, the governmentality studies' critique of restorative justice centres on restorative justice as both a disciplinary technique and as a technology of self, which together contribute to the deployment of restorative justice as a mode of neoliberal governmentality.

The disciplinary components of restorative justice are particularly evident in meetings conducted by 'governmentalist' restorative justice organisations. Such organisations, for instance, are more likely to employ coercive strategies to ensure wrongdoer repentance during restorative justice encounters. Thus, co-ordinators for such programmes might threaten a reluctant wrongdoer with the strictures of the formal justice system if he or she refuses to participate in a restorative encounter. Governmentalist programmes are also more likely to use semi-adjudicative techniques such as 'community accountability panels' to deal with wrongdoings (Woolford and Ratner, 2003). For example, in England and Wales, referral orders given under the Youth Justice and Criminal Evidence Act 1999 allow courts to direct young offenders to a youth offender panel, comprised of two trained community members and a representative from the official Youth Offender Team. This panel, after hearing from the youth and perhaps other stakeholders (for example, victims and family members) will, in co-operation with the youth, devise an agreement consisting of remedial activities to be completed by the youth over the duration of the remedial order (Crawford and Newburn, 2002). Although drawing upon the principles of restorative justice, such as Braithwaite's (1989) notion of 'reintegrative shaming', these panels are nevertheless relatively formal in the sense that the offending youth is confronted with three authoritative community members who work to ensure that she is held accountable for her wrongdoing. Such panels are also beset with managerialist concerns in respect of the cost and time savings expected by government funders, which may encourage panel members to reduce more time-consuming restorative justice interventions and to engage in evaluative decision making. In this manner, the accountability panel risks taking on characteristics of what Garfinkel (1956) refers to as 'degradation' ceremonies, in that they might become public shaming events that serve to stigmatise wrongdoers. If the panel is too condemnatory in its interactions with a young offender, it is unlikely that the young offender or her supporters will possess the social power or communicative capacity to challenge the authority of the community notables, thus making their public stigmatisation of the young offender more acute.

The disciplinary power of community accountability panels is here quite evident. Using the social power invested in the panel members, the panels serve to reshape offender conduct through the moral authority of respected community members. Moreover, these panel members are not simply surrogates for state power; instead, they represent a more diffuse form of social power that filters throughout society and is invested in informal agents who serve on local community accountability panels. In this manner, disciplinary force as implemented through restorative justice encounters is not necessarily the direct result of the actions of official state actors. But it should be noted that, within governmentalist restorative justice programmes, it is not uncommon to have state agents directly involved as is the case in some conferencing programmes that use police officers, trained in the techniques of restorative justice, to manage restorative encounters. These police officers are expected to bracket their official status as agents of the state and, instead, to participate as concerned community members—but it is unlikely that public perceptions of their status as state officials will disappear so easily. Moreover, as Young (2003) notes, police facilitators often draw upon formal authority in subtle ways, such as by defending or explaining police actions when they come under criticism, or by drawing on official police reports as 'facts' within restorative justice encounters. Police-led restorative justice encounters in England and Australia have also shown an inability to protect offenders from stigmatising forms of shaming (Young, 2003).

It is also the case that 'communitarian' forms of restorative justice feature disciplinary moments. While communitarian practitioners of restorative justice are less bound to the conventional goals of governmentalist restorative justice—namely, ensuring the maintenance of public order through the prevention of recidivism and promotion of victim satisfaction—and are more willing to let the end results of restorative justice emerge through the restorative encounter, there are still clear behavioural expectations that guide communitarian restorative justice. The cues used by communitarian facilitators to instil discipline may also be gentler than those used by governmentalist facilitators; nonetheless, they still operate to promote specific forms of conduct. Thus, the communitarian facilitator, in her efforts to encourage productive discussion, will actively discourage all forms of non-communicative behaviour. Participants who monopolise the discussion will be encouraged to make room for others to speak. Participants who show anger or frustration will be asked to express these feelings in a respectful manner and offenders who dissemble, deny responsibility or cast blame will be called upon to be accountable for their actions. None of these interventions are as intrusive as those used in governmentalist restorative justice programmes, but they do represent an attempt to fashion non-disputing and communicative subjects for purposes of maximising the potential for resolution within the restorative justice encounter. Indeed, it is the 'caring' or 'pastoral' nature of the communitarian facilitator's interventions that provides the moral force with which participants are to be convinced that they should model more communicatively productive behaviour (Pavlich, 1999).

These more subtle disciplinary interventions overlap with, and blend into, restorative technologies of self. Non-disputing and peaceable identities are not formed solely through the efforts of restorative justice facilitators; these qualities must also be internalised by participants willing to work upon themselves in order to become less combative in their interactions. Thus, participants are engaged in a project of self-formation set within the normative parameters of restorative justice. In telling their stories about the harmful event, in listening to other perspectives on the consequences of this event and through participating in an effort to resolve this harm, participants are asked repeatedly to articulate who they are and what needs they possess. Moreover, this self-reflective activity is not simply a matter of uncovering an authentic, self-possessing, pre-formed feeling about harm and its resolution; it is rather a process of self-constitution in the face of the moral prescriptions of restorative justice. For example, victims might 'discover' that what they need is not to see the offender punished through incarceration, but rather a sense of security that they will not be harmed again by the same offender. They may also discover that an apology from the offender helps them to recover personal dignity as much as having the state officially vindicate their perspective that they have suffered a grievous wrong. These 'discoveries' are facilitated by restorative justice processes that extend the limits of what is thinkable in relation to criminal justice, by opening new options that allow victims to reconstitute themselves as reasonable and conciliatory people who merely require that their basic interests in safety and dignity should be met, rather than that punishment should be meted out. Indeed, the willingness to undertake this sort of self-work is often a prerequisite to participation in restorative justice programmes. For example, in most programmes, an offender will not be admitted unless he has accepted responsibility for the harm caused. Because restorative justice is not designed to determine guilt or innocence, the offender's admission of responsibility is a logical starting point for restorative encounters; this admission is also intended to signify that the offender is willing to critically examine and change his behaviour. Similarly, restorative justice facilitators will often screen other participants—for example, victims and community members—to ensure that they have the potential to be accepting, or even forgiving, of the offender. These characteristics indicate that they are ready to enter upon a path of 'healing' rather than continuing to hold onto fearful and stigmatising views of the offender.

Both governmentalist and communitarian restorative justice programmes provide opportunities for the application of technologies of self, but these are more active in the less authoritative contexts of communitarian programmes. Governmentalist practitioners of restorative justice are typically more insistent that offenders undertake moral work upon themselves, refusing them any opportunity to lessen or to divert responsibility. Victims are less likely to receive the same encouragement toward using technologies of self, because their role, if any, is merely to add another voice that demands offender accountability and pressures the offender to reform and undertake remedial actions. In contrast, communitarian restorative justice programmes draw upon the 'force of community' (Pavlich, 2001) to persuade both victims and offenders to manage their behaviour in accordance with community-based normative prescriptions. For instance, Anderson (1999, p 310) examines how restorative justice for aboriginal peoples within Canada draws upon an ideal of 'peaceful living' in an imagined past to provide a framework through which Aboriginal Peoples can refashion themselves in accordance with allegedly traditional, non-conflictive norms. The issue here, however, is not only that the tradition drawn upon is not always historically accurate; it is more a matter that this logic is set within colonial relations that deny aboriginal sovereignty and autonomy, yet employ ostensibly aboriginal cultural principles to effect harmony within communities still reeling under the impact of colonialism. Thus, there is a convenient cynicism potentially at work here, promoting conciliatory self-constituting practices that make aboriginal people more governable as (post-)colonial subjects (Anderson, 1999).

In essence, the combination of disciplinary techniques and technologies of self in restorative justice connects it to the ethos of neoliberal governmentality. In particular, restorative justice provides a potential vehicle for carrying governmentality into localities and responsibilising individuals, through the force of their own decisions, to remake themselves as peaceful and accepting community members. According to governmentality scholars, the participatory nature of restorative justice practices provides utilisable fora for the diffusion of a discourse of self-management in the face of increasing social inequities. For example, Pavlich examines four 'frames' that are employed by restorative justice governmentalities:

1.   the object of governance (harm);
2.   visions of who is governed;
3.   the designated governors; and
4.   indications of what appropriate governance entails.

(2005, p 11)

First, restorative justice governmentalities identify a new object of govern-ance, the harm resulting from crime, which is said to be distinct from a formal criminal justice emphasis on a limited, legalistic notion of crime. Second, restorative justice governmentalities widen the scope of who is involved in the criminal conflict, allowing for broader community, victim and offender participation. Third, restorative justice governmentalities seek to take governance from the hands of state and professional actors, and place it instead squarely in the hands of communities. Finally, restorative justice gov-ernmentalities attempt to establish processes that allow stakeholders collect-ively to decide future relations, based upon non-dominated dialogue. Despite the restorative justice presumption that these four elements amount to an empowering alternative to criminal justice, Pavlich argues that they are still founded upon the logic of criminal justice, often imitating, rather than trans-forming, its rationality. For instance, by relying on basic concepts such as 'crime', 'victim' (who is produced in the aftermath of crime) and 'offender', restorative justice is still tied to a criminal justice mode of thinking about conflict and therefore helps to reproduce its hegemony.

Following this view, governmentality scholars contend that restorative just-ice represents not a break from dominant patterns of criminal justice, but instead the rearrangement of criminal justice practices and the redeployment of criminal justice concepts to facilitate the inculcation of responsible, self-governing dispositions. It is therefore the obverse of formal criminal justice governmentalities that use the resources of the state to discipline and consti-tute social behaviour. For Pavlich, this indebtedness to formal criminal justice ultimately deadens the promise of restorative justice:

> So long as restorative justice defines itself through systems of difference that defer to basic criminal justice assumptions, thereby entrenching its dependence on the latter, the degree to which it is able to exceed such assumptions is unduly truncated. This suggests again that an alter-native calculation of justice need not position itself as a servant of state criminal justice decrees.

(2005, p 110)

Thus, the empowering and liberatory prospects of restorative justice are dim, because it is too embedded within existing criminal justice arrangements.

In this way, Pavlich strikes upon a critical insight and correctly alerts restorative justice advocates to the dangers of a justice alternative that is built upon compromised foundations. Instead, he proposes a justice that pushes beyond criminal justice's 'conceptual horizons' and 'calculates' justice in a manner that is free from criminal justice precepts (Pavlich, 2005, pp 106, 116). Pavlich's effort is to provide critical deconstructive tools to help us to think beyond the informal–formal justice complex. He does not, however, attempt to provide a political or institutional framework for realising 'justice anew', which is an essential task if we wish to build upon our critical inquiries a pragmatic means for attempting social change.

In sum, the governmentality studies' critique of restorative justice provides an important perspective on the diffuse nature of power within the informal–formal justice complex and on how the existence of this power makes problematic some of the stronger claims made by restorative justice advocates. Its critical interrogation of restorative justice requires a political programme if we want to move beyond critique, toward strategising the disruption of the informal–formal justice complex so as to challenge its prevailing patterns of neoliberal and professional domination.

Communicative action and restorative justice

Within the restorative justice literature, several authors draw connections between restorative justice and the work of Habermas (Hudson, 2003; Olson and Dzur, 2004; Presser, 2004). This is particularly evident in discussions of the democratic nature of restorative justice (Crawford, 2003; Dzur and Olson, 2004; Parkinson and Roche, 2004). The most notable example of the latter is the republican theory of criminal justice suggested by Braithwaite and Petit (1990; see also Braithwaite, 2002; Braithwaite and Daly, 1994; Walgrave, 2002). This perspective centres on the notion of 'dominion', which refers to the rights and freedoms assured to citizens of democratic societies. 'Domination', in contrast, refers to incursions upon these rights and therefore represents the primary form of social harm that is to be minimised within justice contexts. It is the state's role to create opportunities for dominion and to minimise the likelihood of domination. In respect of restorative justice, this entails the state acting to maintain constitutional space that allows for non-dominated informal justice practices. This does not mean that we can simply discard the authority of formalism in favour of informal practices; instead, informalism and formalism co-exist in a mutually support-ive relationship, each lending their influence to the other. For example, restorative justice might provide citizens with the chance to interact and to address harms within their community, but this is done within legal limits enforced by the state, which ensures that the rights of each party to the restorative justice encounter are respected and intervenes when they are not.

Braithwaite and Petit's perspective shares similarities with the Habermasian vision of communicative action and discourse ethics, in the sense that it affirms the need for a reconstructed institutional order that maximises the potential of local decision making and communicative engagements. In both theories, emphasis is placed on enabling non-coerced, or non-dominated, communication between involved parties in the aftermath of a criminal event. In his discussion of restorative justice standards, Braithwaite (2002) points to similarities between his project and that put forward by Habermas, acknowledging the necessity of some form of top-down accountability to ensure that restorative justice is consistent with human rights standards. Moreover, he contends that these standards must be challengeable from below, as well as adaptable to local circumstances.

The Habermasian influence on restorative justice has become more pronounced in recent years, through discussions of deliberative democracy. Dzur and Olson (2004, p 99), for instance, note that there are 'close resemblances between restorative justice ideals and deliberative democratic ideals of public participation and reasoned value-oriented debate in political forums'. Furthermore, they draw on Habermas' (1999) discussion of the relationship between 'civil society' and the 'public sphere' to illustrate how both restorative justice and deliberative democracy are attuned to public discussion that takes place outside the formal institutions of the state. Finally, they draw on the work of deliberative democrats such as Habermas, Benhabib (1996), Fishkin (1991) and Dryzek (2000), suggesting that these authors provide a clearer sense than do restorative justice theorists of how justice discussions should be conducted in order to enhance their communicative potential. Dzur and Olson (2004) contend that restorative justice might follow deliberative democracy in the establishment of basic guidelines or norms, similar to Habermas' communicative presuppositions discussed in Chapter 2, which direct participants in deliberative settings toward rational, respectful and consistent discussion. Moreover, they argue that such guidelines provide a means for assessing the communicative potential of restorative justice by identifying the places where it fails to live up to the ideals of deliberative democracy. In this regard, they point to coercive and unequal moments within restorative justice encounters, during which offenders are intimidated into participation through the threat of formal judicial action, or victims' voices and accounts are privileged over those of offenders. For Dzur and Olson, it is necessary that 'progressive' restorative justice advocates seek to improve the communicative potential of restorative justice by measuring restorative justice encounters against the ideals of deliberative democracy, so that they can better ensure open and fair participation.

Elsewhere, Olson and Dzur (2004) tackle the question of professional involvement in restorative justice. They suggest that it is not inevitable that professional involvement in restorative justice would result in the co-optation or dilution of restorative values. What matters is how these professionals conduct themselves—whether they fall prey to the hegemonic presuppositions of neoliberal domination and the competitive conditions within the juridical field, or seek instead to act as conduits between public participation and the state. For Olson and Dzur, professionals should claim the latter role:

> Democratic professionals seek to open up their domains of authority to lay participants, to share tasks, and to share in the construction of norms that constrain and direct professional action.
>
> (2004, p 151)

In this sense, their notion of the democratic restorative justice professional is similar to the role that Habermas envisions for law as a bridge between life-world and system. Professionals, according to Olson and Dzur, should act as messengers carrying everyday insights and experiences, drawn from participatory publics, to powerful individuals who are able to act on these local concerns. But it is not solely altruism that motivates this sort of professional involvement. Olson and Dzur suggest that professionals also possess self-interested motivation for exhibiting what they call 'democratic professionalism' (2004, pp 147–54):

- they gain a sense of professional integrity;
- it helps to maintain their professional legitimacy in the eyes of the general public;
- there is a growing awareness of the benefits of democracy over the rigidity of technocratic authority. Thus, the deliberative discourse of restorative justice is not merely a matter of local decision making restricted to local criminal justice issues—it is a means by which public discussion can arise and influence broader institutional patterns.

John Parkinson and Declan Roche (2004) also contribute to the discussion of the applicability of deliberative democracy theory to the practice of restorative justice. Like Dzur and Olson, Parkinson and Roche use the theory of deliberative democracy to evaluate the communicative and political potential of restorative justice. They describe restorative justice as 'a vibrant, grass-roots example of deliberation in practice' (2004, p 506), but add that actual restorative justice encounters experience difficulty in meeting some of the standards of deliberative democracy. Parkinson and Roche identify these standards as inclusiveness, equality between participants, transformative power, scope and decisiveness, and accountability. First, although, in theory, restorative justice programmes promote the inclusion of all parties affected by crime, they are hard pressed to involve all individuals who may have some stake in the outcome, because the ramifications of crime are quite widespread (for example, the fear of crime). Second, the fact that restorative justice encounters are conducted in the shadow of the formal justice system makes problematic the claim that restorative justice promotes equality between participants, because at least one of the participants (the offender) faces the threat of state action if the restorative encounter is unsuccessful. Third, Parkinson and Roche do see a transformative power in restorative justice, but this is not a power that accomplishes individual or social change simply through the *rationality* of stronger arguments made within deliberative contexts; instead, it is the *emotional* force of face-to-face engagement that makes restorative justice a potent source for changing individual views and outlooks. Fourth, they argue that restorative justice does, in fact, widen the scope of democratic participation and offers real decision-making power to the citizenry. Finally, Parkinson and Roche contend that restorative justice programmes and measures might be more accountable if they 'were themselves the result of democratic deliberation rather than the fiat of a few policy makers' (2004, p 515). In sum, they suggest that restorative justice is a potentially valuable form of deliberation, but one that might be improved through further engagement with theoretical insights drawn from the deliberative democracy literature.

While the communicative potential of restorative justice has been widely discussed by restorative justice advocates, it is still not clear how this 'democratic' practice might escape the pressures described by governmentality scholars. Rose (1996), for example, argues that the practices of freedom are entwined with the operations of power, thus suggesting that even seemingly democratic choices are made within a limiting field of power. A Habermasian response might be that public deliberations provide the opportunity for self-correction of the effects of power through the critical discourses of interacting parties, but it is still unclear how actors within the informal–formal justice complex might discover the critical insight necessary to challenge the governmentalisation of restorative justice. In other words, why should we assume that deliberative restorative justice encounters would be spaces for critical interaction and not simply re-enactments of consent to the dominant social order (Fraser, 1997)? Even discussions held in open and non-coercive settings offer no guarantee that we will not simply reproduce dominant societal standards.

Nonetheless, important lessons have been drawn from the existing research on discourse ethics, communicative action and restorative justice. Above all, these authors recognise that restorative justice is situated within an institutional context and that efforts are needed to increase the ability of informal publics to influence system-level activities. They also offer pragmatic models for evaluating attempts to facilitate democratic discussion within restorative justice encounters, which provides a possible means for improving the political and communicative efficacy of restorative justice within the constraints of the informal–formal justice complex.

The prospects for restorative justice in the informal–formal justice complex

Once again, we see a clear tension between the participatory empowerment claims made by restorative justice proponents and the diffusion of power through restorative justice channels identified by governmentality studies critics. In our typification of restorative justice types, however, we have only identified certain restorative justice programmes as being fully governmentalist in their orientation. The other 'communitarian' programmes, although also at risk of complicity in a governmentalist project, are not as deeply immersed in neoliberal logics of governance and therefore may be more able to mobilise effective communicative action within the informal–formal justice complex.

As with mediation in Chapter 3, it is necessary that we consider these forms of restorative justice within the wider contexts of power that have serious ramifications for its transformative promise. Thus, once again, we will reference three sites, or levels, of power in order to assess the disruptive and communicative potential of restorative justice within the informal–formal justice complex:

- broader systems of power;
- power relations within the criminal justice field;
- power relations within the subfield of restorative justice.

First, as an ascendant and pervasive economic and political rationality, neoliberalism affects the communicative potential of restorative justice. As is suggested by the governmentality studies' critique of restorative justice, restorative responses to crime are consistent with neoliberal approaches to governance, in the sense that they provide a means by which to shape individual behaviour through creating conditions in which individuals are encouraged to make 'free' choices in a manner that 'empowers' them to manage their own well-being in accordance with neoliberal precepts. That is, restorative justice offers a pastoral environment in which actors are subtly trained to take on non-disputive identities that represent the internalisation of governance. This form of identification is the basis for the 'normal' social relations envisioned in both restorative and neoliberal ideals—peaceable and productive communities capable of taking care of their own problems and of adapting to various social challenges.

This ethical overlap between neoliberalism and restorative justice can then be further exploited as the neoliberal regimes that fund restorative justice programmes make specific demands of, or place constraints upon, how restorative justice plays its governmentalising role. It is under these conditions that communitarian restorative justice programmes find it exceedingly difficult to maintain values and practices that are more open-ended, and less legally and economically 'rational', than neoliberal governments would like. Any programme seeking to pursue outcomes different from those typically prescribed by neoliberal governments—for example, lowered rates of recidivism and lower costs of justice—are likely to find themselves at a competitive disadvantage in terms of obtaining government funding (Presser, 2004). Thus, a programme oriented toward providing public opportunities to discuss and transform the way we think about and practise justice is unlikely to produce the measurable outcomes that appeal to neoliberal governments. Moreover, because its goals would have more to do with the creation of dialogue about harm (which would likely transcend any particular criminal event) than the reduction of crime, it would hold less immediate benefits for these governments. With the dismantling of the social welfare state (Wacquant, 2001), neoliberal governments are restructuring the social world in a manner that deprives restorative justice programmes of the supportive services that they require in order to effect change for victim and offenders. As welfare services are rolled back, restorative justice loses access to services that might help restorative justice clients to reform their lives. In this sense, no matter what the more progressive goals of restorative justice programmes may be with regard to increasing participation and providing opportunities for personal and social transformation, neoliberalism narrows and isolates these efforts, restricting their activities to that of local problem solving in the aftermath of crime.

Neoliberalism has, indeed, had a significant impact on the second level of our analysis: power relations within the criminal justice field. While, on the one hand, neoliberal criminal justice has brought back punitive forms of criminal justice, as law-and-order politicians have been able to capitalise on forms of 'tough justice' such as 'three strikes' laws and 'chain gangs' (Pratt, 2002), on the other hand, it has fostered the expansion of so-called informal justice methods, such as community and restorative justice. This reflects the growing entrenchment of the informal–formal justice complex, which permits a flexible rationality of justice that adapts to specific circumstances, and applies justice strategies according to an assessment of the political and economic stakes of certain forms of crime, as well as taking into account local demands for justice. Thus, it may be that restorative justice is touted by government as an ideal way to respond to youth crime, with the exception that certain violent crimes or repeat offences call for greater retributive action on the part of the state. Such a bifurcated justice system allows for the conservation of state resources and a reduction of state interventions in some cases, but also for their redeployment toward those crimes deemed most socially serious and for which public outcry would likely follow any lenient treatment.

Power relations within the field of criminal justice also impact more directly on restorative justice through the involvement of criminal justice professionals in restorative practices and the prevalence of retributive thinking within contemporary society. As stated above, restorative justice is unable to function without assistance from the resources and personnel of the state. Restorative justice is also linked discursively to the criminal justice system, because it takes for granted many of its baseline notions: for example, crime, victim and offender (Pavlich, 2005). In this manner, it is strongly entwined in the relations of the informal–formal justice complex. This is not to say that criminal justice professionals simply espouse criminal justice principles when they are involved in restorative justice encounters. Although this does happen in some circumstances (Young, 2003), in others, professionals have shown an ability to buy into the spirit of restorative justice encounters and to participate as citizens rather than as authorities (Shapland et al, 2006). Rather, it is an acknowledgement that there are criminal justice presuppositions already operational in the lexicon of restorative justice practices; consequently, there are many opportunities for criminal justice reasoning to infiltrate and determine restorative justice practice. Finally, because restorative justice is situated necessarily in the shadow of the criminal justice system, the threat of the punitive system always looms and, to some extent, conditions deliberative discussions within restorative encounters.

Third, restorative justice is itself expanding as a justice market and this has various consequences. On the one hand, restorative justice advocates vie for positions as charismatic leaders of the movement and seek personal fulfilment through the spread of restorative justice values. On the other hand, many diversionary programmes are rebranding themselves as restorative justice in order to profit off the moral capital that derives from this label. Between these charismatic and instrumentalist extremes, we find a diversity of individuals seeking a niche within the restorative justice market. While restorative justice has been less prone to the credentialing and professionalising strategies evident in civil mediation, it is nonetheless the case that there exists a great deal of competition within the restorative justice market. Moreover, because the stakes of this market are, for the most part, state funding and access to state criminal caseloads, the market tends to advantage those governmentalist and instrumental appropriations of restorative justice values that are most willing to accommodate neoliberal agendas.

Despite the influence of these broader levels of power, democratic and empowering moments can arise within both governmentalist and communitarian restorative justice practices. These moments are undoubtedly fewer in governmentalist encounters in which the emphasis is placed on responsibilising the offender so as to ensure future conformist behaviour, but an open-minded and responsive governmentalist facilitator might provide the offender with the opportunity to speak honestly and be heard in respect of what led to the criminal incident in the first place. In such circumstances, for example, a young offender might experience, for the first time, being heard by adults and having these adults truly consider the validity of his presentation. This may provide the youth with a sense of efficacy that would allow him to feel more confident in his interactions.

In communitarian restorative justice, one would expect such democratic and empowering experiences to be the norm. More emphasis is placed here on involving all stakeholders—namely, victims, offenders and community members—and on providing them with the opportunity to speak to the matter at hand. Moreover, these participants are encouraged to address the conflict in its broader social context, rather than focus narrowly on the criminal event as an isolated and disconnected phenomenon. Thus, ideally, each party will feel empowered to raise concerns, to bring matters to the table, whether or not they are 'admissible' in a strictly legal sense, and to propose solutions to the problem that stretch beyond normal juridical sanctions, perhaps even including proposals for broader changes to be made within the community. Indeed, these considerations and suggestions might even be of a critical type that question the very terms of criminal justice and position the conflict in an entirely different light. Such a discussion would mark a significant democratic opportunity for participants to speak to the immediate case before them and to wider problems in the community, and any collective response they could actualise, based upon these discussions, would augment a sense of political agency.

But the problem of sustaining these empowering moments rears its ugly head once more. Most restorative justice programmes, whether governmentalist or communitarian, are not resourced to levels that allow them to guarantee the implementation of democratically established resolutions or to give greater voice to disruptive insights discovered within restorative justice encounters. Indeed, restorative justice programmes often have difficulty actualising even the most mundane recommendations that derive from these encounters. For example, if a restorative justice encounter arrives at a decision that a young offender needs to attend anger management sessions, requires drug counselling and should abide by an 8 pm curfew, such a resolution is only realisable if there are places available for the young offender in anger management and drug counselling programmes, and if a guardian, parent or caseworker is able to supervise the youth to ensure that he obeys his curfew. Most restorative justice programmes do not offer these services in-house and therefore rely on other community organisations to provide them. It can be very difficult to judge, within a spontaneous restorative justice session, how long a wait there might be for a spot to open up in a particular rehabilitative programme and the momentum of empowerment may be lost if nothing comes available until several months after the restorative agreement has been reached.

In a period during which social services are being eroded and neoliberal rationalities are gaining hegemonic status, it becomes increasingly difficult to sustain the empowering moments provided by restorative justice. Even if restorative justice were to be practised in a manner that encourages critical and deconstructive discussions of the criminal justice status quo, there would still be the challenge of affording political opportunities for the wider dissemination and institutional application of such insights. Without a political strategy that extends beyond the confines of the restorative encounter, the restorative justice movement—in both its governmentalist and communitarian forms—will likely be unable to provide substantive justice to those involved in criminal events. What is needed is an institutional means for enabling a broader resonance of insights that are democratically constituted within interactive restorative contexts. But before we address this important question, we must first visit our final research site: reparations.

Conclusion

To summarise, in this chapter, we have:

- briefly discussed competing definitions of restorative justice;
- examined claims that restorative justice reflects an 'ancient' way of doing justice;
- outlined the recent resurgence of restorative justice practices and their acceptance by, and implementation within, Western formal criminal justice systems;
- noted criticisms of the dangers that restorative justice will be co-opted and professionalised, alienating it from its social justice roots;
- identified two ideal types of restorative justice—governmentalist and communitarian—with the former term representing those programmes that assist in the reproduction of the dominant normative order through strategies of offender and community responsibilisation, and the latter referring to those programmes that seek a largely community-based means for locally defined social justice;
- drawn upon the governmentality studies' critique of restorative justice to discuss how techniques of discipline and technologies of self operate within restorative practices;
- highlighted key attempts to employ insights from discourse ethics and the theory of communicative action, to improve the practice of restorative justice and to guide the restorative justice movement toward establishing more effective deliberative encounters;
- initiated a reconceptualisation of restorative justice as a practice embedded within the informal–formal justice complex and subject to various levels of social power. The purpose of this exercise was to highlight the many obstacles facing restorative justice and that prevent it, in some cases, from achieving citizen empowerment, and, in encounters during which empowering moments occur, from sustaining these moments beyond that restorative encounter. This analysis will inform our discussion in Chapter 6, in which we present the rudiments of a political strategy for reinvigorating the notion of transformative informal justice.

Chapter 5

Reparations in the informal–formal justice complex

In this chapter, we seek to define the field of reparations politics and to illustrate its claims to informality. We also trace the history of reparations politics as it has developed, through the efforts of victim movements to achieve recompense and justice, alongside the efforts of states to establish societal stability in the aftermath of mass violence. We also discuss the concerns expressed by prominent scholars who see new forms of state control and professional domination potentially resulting from reparations politics. This leads us to draw an ideal-typical distinction between two forms of reparations politics: one that is driven by demands for the reconfiguration of social, economic and political structures deemed to have caused historical injustices (transformative reparations), and another that is grounded in limited efforts to recompense victims in order to perpetuate the prevailing social order (affirmative reparations). Finally, we explore insights from governmentality studies and the theories of communicative action and discourse ethics to situate reparations within the informal–formal justice complex, enabling an assessment of the prospects for transformative reparations.

The field of reparations politics consists of various methods for coming to terms with mass violence. In the aftermath of state oppression, civil and international war, genocide and other forms of sustained mass violence, remedies are often sought to foster healing at the individual, community and national levels. Trials and tribunals—such as the International Military Tribunal at Nuremberg, which was implemented following World War II to try Nazi war criminals—represent a formal approach to past injustices. Their primary function is to create juridical mechanisms through which leaders and perpetrators can be held accountable for their roles in atrocities and other deadly abuses. But, in recent years, other options, such as truth commissions, have been developed for societies looking to contend with historical injustices. Typically, truth commissions are officially sanctioned, but informally operated, temporary bodies that conduct public hearings about, and research into, patterns of abuse that occurred within a specified historical period (Hayner, 2002). In what is arguably the most high-profile example, the South African Truth and Reconciliation Commission (SATRC), the commission was divided into three parts: an amnesty committee, to which former perpetrators could apply and, upon full admission of their political crimes, receive an official reprieve; a human rights committee, which heard, from survivors and victims' families, their experiences of gross human rights violations[1] committed under the apartheid regime; a reparation and rehabilitation committee, which was charged with the task of recommending symbolic and material forms of redress to be made available to victims of gross human rights violations.

With this latter committee, the South African TRC overlaps with a second informal response to past injustices: compensation.[2] By 'compensation', we mean specifically monetary payment and payments in kind made to victim groups in the aftermath of mass violence. Monetary payments may be made individually, collectively, or both. Individual payments, in many cases, derive from an actuarial assessment of the physical and emotional harm suffered by a specific person, but others consist of a lump-sum payment intended to symbolise government regret for past harmful actions.[3] Collective compensation, in contrast, is paid to a group as a form of general atonement for harmful actions taken against all, or most, of its members. Payments in kind may include the provision of goods and services in lieu of monetary compensation, such as the establishment of educational programmes or health services for a previously marginalised group.

Compensation should be understood separately from a third alternative to tribunals: restitution. Unlike compensation, which attempts to place either a symbolic or actual value on suffering, 'restitution' simply means the return of wealth and goods taken from groups targeted through mass violence and other injustices. Mass violence, it should be noted, rarely involves just violence, because theft of resources is one motivation that leaders use to foment public participation in events such as massacres and ethnic cleansing (Jones, 2006). Thus, in these situations, it is not simply a matter of perpetrators exterminating or expelling targeted groups: they also lay claim to their homes, possessions, jobs and monetary wealth. Once the violence has subsided, it is sometimes possible to return these goods to their rightful owners.

It is not always the case, however, that reparations are conducted entirely through the redistribution of material goods. Indeed, groups targeted by mass violence also seek recognition in the form of symbolic politics, a fourth alternative to trials. By 'symbolic politics', we mean actions taken by a current

---

1 This focus on 'gross human rights violations' led the Truth and Reconciliation Commission to ignore the more widespread, but legal, harms of South African apartheid, such as the Pass Laws and the Population Registration and Group Areas Acts, which respectively restricted economic opportunities for blacks and divided families (see Mamdani, 2000).
2 As we note later in the chapter, compensation has recently been pursued increasingly through the courts, but our focus here is upon compensation that is informally negotiated between former adversaries.
3 In this respect, compensation clearly overlaps with what we refer to as 'symbolic politics'.

regime to signal that it acknowledges past wrongs and is making an effort to ensure that these horrific events are not repeated. The most frequent expressions of symbolic politics are statements of regret or apology. Several collective apologies have been made in recent years, including one by Queen Elizabeth on behalf of the British Empire to the Maori peoples of New Zealand and a statement of regret issued by the Canadian government for its treatment of Aboriginal Peoples, specifically with regards to the residential schooling system (see Tavuchis, 1991; Brooks, 1999).[4]

Finally, a fifth alternative takes the form of what Torpey (2006) refers to as acts of 'communicative history'. These acts include a variety of means for commemorating an unsavoury past. Initially, efforts made to encourage public memory may be completely informal, taking the form of journalistic and literary treatments of wrongful events or public demonstrations. Such activities may, however, be followed by the establishment of days of remembrance and public memorials, by changes to school curricula and texts that acknowledge historical injustices, and by broader efforts to encourage public consciousness of the past. Museums, such as the US Holocaust Memorial Museum in Washington DC, have also become increasingly popular tools for the raising of public consciousness.

Few of these so-called informal alternatives occur in a space that is fully separate from the realm of formal power. Each, in its own way, requires state assistance to implement its reparative strategy publicly. Truth commissions, if they are to gain public attention, state funding and access to official records, must receive official state support. Compensation, symbolic politics and restitution are measures that are most often implemented by states and their administrative systems. And communicative history usually depends on state assistance, at least for commemorative efforts such as days of remembrance, memorials and changes to school curricula. So what, if anything, allows us to consider these justice processes to be informal? As with mediation and restorative justice, we do not suggest that these processes are entirely informal. Like these two other types of so-called informal justice, reparations are lodged within the informal–formal justice complex, in that they are embedded within a complementary and mutually reinforcing relationship with formal justice practices. But also, like mediation and restorative justice, they present greater opportunities for informal and unscripted communicative moments to arise in the aftermath of perceived collective injustices. In other words, they allow public communication about, and input into, justice and thus represent dialogical settings in which matters might be decided through deliberative, rather than adjudicative, processes.

---

4 Questions about the sincerity of such apologies and statements of regret often arise. For example, some aboriginal persons viewed the Canadian statement of regret as a carefully hedged and largely meaningless statement.

A brief history of reparations

Ancient roots?

Unlike restorative justice and mediation, reparations are typically represented as a modern phenomenon. Indeed, until recently, the term 'reparations', when used in relation to war and mass violence, referred to payments made by defeated nations to the victors upon the cessation of military conflict. Post-conflict justice, then, was a matter for states, not victims. In this sense, this is not a case of states 'stealing' justice, to draw on Christie's (1977) expression once again; rather, states have always jealously guarded post-war justice, with victor states claiming the spoils of war, while victims and combatants were left to recover from war's excesses.

In the twentieth century—the so-called 'Age of Genocide' (Alvarez, 2001; Power, 2002; Smith, 1987)—we also see the dawning of victim claims to post-war and post-atrocity justice. This begins roughly with the genocide of Armenians in Turkey in 1915.[5] Humiliated and bitter from the shrinking of the Ottoman Empire, and fearful of Armenian complicity with their Russian enemies, the 'Young Turks' of the Committee for Unity and Progress launched a brutal assault on Armenians residing within Turkish borders (Jones, 2006; Mann, 2005). Turkish forces killed Armenian men of fighting age and for-cibly removed the remaining population into the desert, where they were subject to starvation, periodic murderous attacks by brigands, rape and other indignities. In the end, approximately 1.5 million Armenians were killed in a prolonged slaughter that Turkish leaders still refuse to call 'genocide'.

Observers of the genocide called upon the world community to bring it to an end, initiating one of the first movements to address crimes of mass vio-lence (Jones, 2006; Power, 2002). Henry Morganthau, the American Ambas-sador to Turkey, for example, decried Turkish actions and sought to bring the tragedy to international attention. His efforts, and those of others, led to numerous publications in the *New York Times* and other media outlets that exposed the genocide as it was happening. The public outcry that resulted eventually convinced the Allies to try the leaders of the genocide, charging them with 'crimes against humanity', but unfolding post-war geopolitics eventually caused the British and other world powers to drop the charges and accept Turkish claims that the atrocities were part of an internal struggle between Turkish armed forces and Armenian rebels. Justice, therefore, was never consummated, leaving retribution in the hands of victims such as Soghomon Tehlirian, who, in 1921, shot Talat Pasha, one of the CUP leaders, in the streets of Berlin (Power, 2002; Jones, 2006).

---

5 International concern was raised about the Belgian 'Rubber Terror' in the Congo in the early part of the twentieth century, but this movement outcry did not culminate in an attempt to address these injustices either formally or informally (Jones, 2006).

It was not until the end of World War II that an international tribunal was established to confront crimes of war and mass violence. This was the afore-mentioned International Military Tribunal (IMT) at Nuremberg, at which 24 Nazi defendants were tried for 'crimes against peace', 'crimes of war', and 'crimes against humanity'.[6] Although some victims had an opportunity to give testimony in this formal setting, the case was primarily built upon the written record. This strategy was facilitated by the fact that the Nazis were meticu-lous record keepers, enabling the Allies to make the trial appear as objective and fact-based as possible, thereby stemming charges of 'victor's justice' and 'retroactivity' (Minow, 1998). In his opening statement to the IMT, Chief Justice Robert Jackson was adamant that the trial represented a rational, rather than vengeful, approach to crimes of mass violence:

> The wrongs which we seek to condemn and punish have been so calcu-lated, so malignant, and so devastating, that civilization cannot tolerate their being repeated. That four great nations, flushed with victory and stung with injury, stay the hand of vengeance and voluntarily submit to the judgment of law is one of the most significant tributes that Power has ever paid to Reason.
>
> (International Military Tribunal, 1995, p 99)

But the lack of victim involvement—in particular, the absence of sufficient testimony from Jewish victims of the Holocaust (Bloxham, 2001)—left many unsatisfied. Although momentary relief might have been provided to victims through the imprisonment or hanging of those found guilty at the IMT and through subsequent trials, these attempts at post-conflict justice did not fully address the healing needs of those who had lost close friends and family members, those who had been forced from their homelands, those who had experienced mental trauma and physical injuries at the hands of the Nazis, and those who had suffered the theft of their possessions and livelihood. In the immediate aftermath of World War II, many of these same victims were too burdened with the demands of existence to pursue a course of reparations politics and the world community seemed uninterested in dwelling on the crimes of the past (Novick, 1999). Yet, despite these barriers to mobilisation, a movement was emerging to demand material and symbolic recompense from Germany.

---

6 The Tokyo Trials were also held in the aftermath of World War II to try Japanese war crim-inals. Subsequent tribunals also took place at Nuremberg and throughout Germany to try legal and medical professionals, and judges, among others (see Bloxham, 2001), but, in the end, very few of those complicit in World War II crimes were brought to justice.

Reparations movements

Even before the end of World War II, Jewish groups had organised to ensure that the Allies would hear their reparation concerns. Although these same groups were simultaneously contending with the exodus of needy refugees from Europe, the vitality of the Jewish reparations debate is reflected in the publication during this period of several monographs articulating the Jewish claim: for example, Robinson's *Indemnification and Reparations* (1944), Moses' *Jewish Post-War Claims* (1944) and Goldschmidt's *Legal Claims Against Germany* (1945). Moreover, organisations were established in London, New York and Jerusalem, among other places, to pursue Jewish reparations demands.

The USA was the country most receptive to these claims and the Jewish reparations organisations found early success following the end of World War II through the 1947 American Military Law No 59, which was implemented in the American zone of West Germany to create a process for the restitution of stolen Jewish property (Military Government of Germany, 1948). This law was soon adapted to the French and British military zones, before it was developed into a common law for all of West Germany in 1949. Jewish reparations organisations viewed these restitution laws to be insufficient, however, because they focused narrowly on the return of Jewish property and ignored the broader harms of the Holocaust.

An opportunity for wider reparations arose in December 1951, when West German Chancellor Konrad Adenauer proclaimed to Parliament that West Germany must address demands for material reparations. Soon thereafter, Adenauer agreed to negotiations with Israel and the newly formed Conference on Jewish Claims Against Germany (or 'Claims Conference'), an umbrella body that represented various Western Jewish organisations. Meetings began in March 1952, in the Dutch town of Wassenaar, and culminated on 10 September 1952, in the Luxembourg Agreement. This agreement featured a lump-sum payment of DM 3bn to Israel (much of this in the form of goods) and also contained two Protocols in respect of the Claims Conference: the first required West Germany to improve existing compensation and restitution legislation, to make it more readily available to a wider group of claimants; the second provided a payment of DM 450m to the Claims Conference (Goschler, 2004).

This reparations agreement did not, however, mean an end to Jewish reparations claims. Despite the agreement's requirements that West Germany improve its restitution legislation, new demands continued to arise in respect of the limitations of West German reparations policy. For example, the 1956 revised Federal Compensation Law improved on the narrow framework of American Military Law No 59, moving West German reparations beyond mere restitution, but it still presented several problems for claimants. First, it restricted claims to those based upon racial, religious or political persecutions, which raised challenges for Roma and Sinti (formerly 'gypsies') claimants who were allegedly persecuted as 'criminals' (Puxon, 1981). Second, only those who lived within the German borders as of 1 December 1937 or who moved to the Federal Republic within certain time limits were permitted to apply, thus restricting reparations largely to those 'who currently were German nationals or who had been German nationals at the time of their persecution by the Nazis' (Goschler, 2004, p 391). Finally, reparations were only available to claimants living in countries that held diplomatic relations with West Germany, thus excluding those victims from Eastern European nations or those who had fled to them (Goschler, 2004; Schrafstetter, 2003). The continued efforts of the Claims Conference resulted in the 1965 'Final Law', a law that was final only in name, because victims excluded from this law pressed for further legislation that would recognise their claims. More recently, the German government has attempted to forge a 'legal peace' in respect of reparations claims through the establishment of the Remembrance, Responsibility and Future Foundation in 2000, which is intended, in particular, to bring an end to US lawsuits against German corporations and the German government.

But German reparations have included more than only monetary payments: German society has, especially since the 1960s, been the site of much discussion about the past in what Charles Maier (1988, p 2) has referred to as a project of 'German national self-interrogation'. In its art, history and politics, German society has reckoned with the Holocaust, as the nation tries to repair a national identity that may be forever tainted by Nazi crimes (Goldhagen, 2003). This sense of historical remorse has resulted in political figures making symbolic acts of atonement, ranging from Chancellor Konrad Adenauer's initial attempt at atonement through monetary payments in 1952, which was viewed by some as a self-serving attempt to restore Germany's international credibility (Barkan, 2000), to Chancellor Willy Brandt falling on his knees in the Warsaw Ghetto to apologise for Nazi atrocities—a more successful action than Adenauer's, because it was perceived to be sincere due to Brandt's historical opposition to the Nazis (Meyer, 1997; see also Tavuchis, 1991).

Although German reparations are not universally praised and some victims still view the payments as 'blood money', the movement to achieve reparations for Jewish victims of the Holocaust is remarkable. It represents the successful mobilisation of numerous Jewish organisations, the state of Israel and public opinion (particularly in the USA and Germany, but also worldwide) to create a surge of support for material and symbolic atonement. It also represents the creative use of multiple formats (formal courts and informal negotiations) and strong political pressure (lobbying, protests, education) to ensure the effective facilitation of reparation demands. Moreover, the movement was able to use the social conditions in Germany—for example, the desire of West Germany to gain acceptance from the international community following the war—to advance its claim. In the end, its efforts allowed for the formation of the Jewish state of Israel, for national atonement in Germany and for a distribution (albeit, in some cases, minimal) of compensation to victims of the Holocaust.

For all of these reasons, the Holocaust has become the 'model' and 'symbol' for subsequent reparations movements (Torpey, 2001). Some groups, such as the Roma and Sinti, tried to build reparations movements based on the Jewish model, making demands for material and symbolic reparations for the genocide committed against them by the Nazis during World War II (that is, the Porrajmos; see Margalit, 2002; Woolford and Wolejszo, 2006). Others, such as the Herero of what is now Namibia, regarded German reparations to Jewish groups as grounds for demanding recompense for the genocide committed by German forces against the Herero people in 1904 (Torpey, 2006). Indeed, even groups that had long been making reparations demands against their former assailants, such as indigenous groups seeking land claims and self-determination, viewed Jewish Holocaust reparations as a source of inspiration and comparison (Woolford, 2005).

By the 1970s, a globalising Holocaust consciousness began to take hold, with novels, films, plays and other media portraying the Holocaust as the height of human evil (Novick, 1999; Cole, 1999). Moreover, alongside the growing resonance and awareness of genocide, a new perspective on victims and victim identities began to emerge (Garland, 2001). The victim identity was no longer perceived as a mark of weakness and passivity; instead, it was infused with a sense of nobility and unchallengeable innocence. More and more, victimised groups began to embrace their victim (or 'survivor') status and to use it as a point around which to mobilise, demanding societal recognition for past sufferings. These movements contributed to the development of a victims' communicative history, as societies strove to commemorate wrongful actions taken against previously despised groups. Memorials, museums, days of remembrance and other symbolic actions became commonplace within Western societies, as governments sought to appease the demands of reparations movements.

The elevation of victims within justice discussions also raised questions about the justice processes employed to deal with the past. The offender-centred justice of the IMT, while satisfying in its clear judgment of perpetrator guilt, provided few other reparative benefits for victims. Moreover, in places such as Guatemala, El Salvador, Argentina and South Africa, it was very difficult to prosecute perpetrators, because these individuals retained considerable power in these 'transitional' societies (see Kritz, 1995; Offe, 1997; Teitel, 2000). Thus, a new breed of justice came to the fore, offering a new 'model' for the world community: the truth commission (see Hayner, 2002). Truth commissions gained international attention when they were employed in several Latin American nations after the fall of dictatorial regimes, but it is the South African Truth and Reconciliation Commission that has gained the widest publicity and which has reshaped popular thought about what justice might mean in a post-conflict context.

The SATRC was the result of a historic compromise. With the end of apartheid and the election of Nelson Mandela's African National Congress into power, discussions began centring on the question of how to bring justice to South Africa. Although there was a desire to hold perpetrators accountable, this posed a serious challenge given that white South Africans still controlled much of the nation's military, as well as other vital institutional resources. An extremely aggressive justice strategy that promised harsh punishment for the architects and perpetrators of apartheid's crimes might well have resulted in civil war (Adam, 2000). For this reason, it was proposed that South Africa adapt the truth commission strategy made popular in Latin America, reworking it so that it would maximise social and political reconciliation. An important component of this reconciliation was that there would be no blanket amnesty for gross human rights violations committed under apartheid, as had been the case with some of the Latin American commissions. Perpetrators would be held accountable under the SATRC, to the extent that they were required to stand before the 'amnesty committee' and tell the full truth of their participation in politically motivated crimes. If the committee found the applicant to be dissembling or manipulating the facts, the applicant could be denied amnesty and brought before the courts either for criminal acts or through a civil lawsuit. Likewise, if a perpetrator refused to stand before the amnesty committee, he too would be open to legal action. It should be noted, however, that the amnesty committee did not require that the perpetrators express remorse or regret for their past actions, only that they tell the truth.

Separate hearings were held for victims of apartheid-era gross human rights violations and it is these hearings that have led some to refer to the SATRC as 'victim-centred' justice (Rigby, 2001, p 6). At these hearings, victims were encouraged to tell their stories, to express their needs, and to receive support and recognition from the community. In this sense, the hearings were meant to be 'cathartic' moments in which the discussion of past events would help victims to begin the healing process (Minow, 1998). Moreover, the stories told within the victim hearings were broadcast via South African TV and reported in the media, making South Africans more aware of the harms caused by apartheid. Finally, the cathartic role of the victim committee was to be complemented by the work of the reparations and reconciliation committee, which was tasked with recommending to the government the material and symbolic reparations that would be offered to victims, as well as the therapeutic services that would be needed to help victims to cope with their trauma.

The SATRC, therefore, represents a state-sponsored, but informally administered, attempt at post-conflict justice. For this reason, it has been hailed as an example of 'restorative justice' (Minow, 1998; Tutu, 2000). It is also viewed as being restorative because it brings together perpetrators, victims and community members—albeit under different roofs through separate committees and through the power of the media—to resolve conflict and create harmony in the aftermath of crime.

Although questions have been raised about the success of the SATRC—in particular, that it has promised too much and delivered too little to victims (Mamdani, 2000)—it has, nevertheless, inspired several recent justice experiments in the aftermath of mass violence. One such experiment is the use of *gacaca* or 'front yard' justice in Rwanda, which was initiated in 2002. Following the Rwandan genocide, Rwandan prisons were severely over-crowded, because neither the Rwandan justice system nor the International Criminal Tribunal for Rwanda could efficiently process the approximately 130,000 accused perpetrators awaiting trial. Indeed, the Rwandan juridical infrastructure was itself a victim of the genocide, with judges, lawyers and other legal professionals in short supply as a result of the killings (Vandeginste, 2003). To address this situation, it was proposed that a traditional form of community justice, the *gacaca*, be used to expedite the justice process and to allow for increased community input into sentencing decisions. At *gacaca* meetings, perpetrators confront their victims in a communal discussion about the perpetrator's crimes. This informal community-based component is, however, combined with Western legal traditions: for example, the *gacaca* model empowers a lay judge to determine the offender's sentence.

Broadly speaking, the current trend in international justice is to attempt to build justice mechanisms that draw on local resources and informal traditions, while, at the same time, meeting the justice standards of the international community. This is a difficult balance to achieve, because experiments such as the *gacaca* are perceived by some to violate principles of fairness and due process (Amnesty International, 2002), and international courts such as the International Criminal Tribunal for the former Yugoslavia at the Hague are too distant from local contexts to educate and reconcile those still trapped in continuing cycles of violence (Minow, 1998). Sierra Leone's reparations process is one attempt to mix requirements, with culturally adapted truth commission procedures working side by side with tribunals that draw upon established international legal principles.

Co-optation and professionalisation

Like restorative justice, reparative responses to mass violence have been criticised for the extent to which they strengthen or renew state control. Reparations, it is argued, can never truly 'repair' crimes of mass violence, nor can they 'restore' its victims. For this reason, reparations may serve as little more than a salve applied by states in an attempt to cover over past injustices, and are often perceived as a disingenuous confrontation with the past. A memorable example of this criticism took the form of a violent protest that erupted within the Israeli Knesset in January 1952, over claims that the Israeli government was accepting 'blood money' from West Germany (Barkan, 2000, p 9). In particular, some critics suspected that the Israeli government was profiting off the suffering of concentration camp victims in order to fund the struggling new nation. Moreover, in so doing, they were perceived to be allowing West Germans to buy their way back into good standing in the international community. Other critics of West German reparations took issue with the amounts paid to survivors, which hardly matched the suffering they experienced (Kim, 1999), as well as with the overly bureaucratic and sometimes re-traumatising application process (Pross, 1998).

John Torpey (2006) has expressed further misgivings about the 'politics' of reparations politics. For Torpey, most reparations claims lack a progressive vision. He asks:

> Is it more than mere coincidence that the proliferation of reparations politics comes on the heels of the collapse of socialism and extensive doubts about the viability of the nation-state?
>
> (2006, p 5)

According to this view, reparations often add up to little more than a venal redistribution of goods and monies: one that reflects the current poverty of our ability to imagine a better alternative. Torpey suggests that, without a sense of a utopian future, we settle for a compensatory justice that threatens to reinforce group differences in a misguided attempt to correct past wrongs. Thus, rather than act as a harbinger of positive social change, reparations politics tends to, at best, maintain the status quo or, at worst, produce essentialised group identities that are likely to trigger future conflicts. Under these terms, reparations can be viewed as a co-opted and corrupted justice practice.

Reparations politics also faces the twin dangers of professionalisation and juridification. Instead of coming about as the result of informal negotiations, as was the case for post-Holocaust reparations, modern reparations are increasingly sought through lawyers and the courts. Torpey (2006) fears that this legalistic trend will reduce reparations to monetary settlements and preclude efforts to raise public consciousness about past injustices. Victim groups have been particularly savvy in using domestic legislation, such as the US Alien Tort Claims Act, to pursue civil claims against perpetrators and against corporations that profited from human rights abuses. For example, reparations lawsuits against Swiss banks, European insurance companies and German corporations for harms relating to the Nazi period have inspired similar lawsuits sponsored by South African victims of apartheid and descendants of American slaves. Contrary to Torpey's view, however, it should be acknowledged that these reparations demands made through formal justice processes have proved a vital tool for victim movements facing unresponsive states that refuse to negotiate an informal resolution. Indeed, they can, in some cases, force governments to the negotiation table, as has happened in Canada where, through a series of court victories, First Nations in the province of British Columbia have forced the federal and provincial governments to negotiate land claims (Tennant, 1990; Woolford, 2005).

Moreover, legal challenges such as these are not entirely without disruptive effect. Because they typically target corporations and government, businesses and government perceive them as a threat to economic stability and certainty. This threat often leaves governments scrambling to close risky legal avenues to reparative justice. In this regard, the South African ANC government, led by president Thabo Mbeki, has rejected and obstructed victim group attempts to seek legal settlements from South African corporations that profited from apartheid. Similarly, the Bush government is attempting to squelch the use of the American Alien Tort Claims Act for the pursuit of reparative justice. In a recent example, US Attorney General John Ashcroft filed an amicus curiae ('friend of the court') brief on behalf of Unocal, in a case involving Burmese slave labourers who were forced by their government to work on a Unocal oil pipeline. The US government makes the argument that the Alien Tort Claims Act was never intended as a tool for enforcing international humanitarian laws (see Human Rights Watch, 2003; *John Doe I et al v Unocal et al*, 2003).

The fragmentation of reparations

Under conditions of co-optation and professionalisation it would seem quite unlikely that reparations politics could be turned toward progressive ends. As noted above, however, reparations politics are not monolithic, but are directed toward a variety of goals, and several analytical distinctions have been made within the reparations literature to highlight differences between reparations processes. These include: commemorative versus anti-systemic reparations (Torpey, 2001; 2003; 2006); reparations as justice-making versus reparations as certainty-making (Woolford, 2005); affirmative versus transformative reparations (Fraser, 1997; Woolford, 2005); reparations versus settlements (Brooks, 2003); reparation as restoration versus reparation as reconciliation (Thompson, 2002).

Several competing dimensions of reparations politics are reflected in these distinctions. First, there is the issue of whether reparations are retrospective or forward-looking. 'Commemorative reparations' and 'reparation as restoration', for example, are said to focus on the past, seeking to correct historical wrongs rather than to fix current injustices, as is more the case for 'anti-systemic reparations' and 'reparation as reconciliation'. Second, with respect to those reparations processes that are forward-looking, questions are raised about the extent to which they seek superficially to address past injustices in order to stabilise and secure an existing social order, or seek to effect a transformation that corrects the social conditions that led to the injustice(s) in the first place.

It is this latter analytical distinction between 'affirmative' and 'transformative' reparations that we take to be the primary fault line in the field of reparations politics. Indeed, it is in respect of this distinction that the *politics* of reparations is most apparent, as parties vie to determine the goals and outcomes of reparations processes. For instance, in cases of blatantly affirmative repair, political actors have engaged in reparations processes to project a concern for justice, but have subsequently ignored the results of their own deliberations. For example, the Zimbabwe Commission of Inquiry was established in 1985 to investigate the government's suppression of so-called dissidents in the Matabeleland region of the country, as well as the deaths of several thousand civilians in the military campaign (Hayner, 2002). The Commission was supported by appropriate auspices (the government, churches and human rights groups), and the format of the Commission seemed suited for raising public awareness about the crimes and for presenting recommendations for reparations.[7] Because the launching of the Commission was President Robert Mugabe's initiative, however, his discretion determined the release of its findings. After giving the impression that he was interested in repair, Mugabe's government chose not to release the Commission's report. As one senior government official put it, 'if you don't talk about it, it may die a natural death, so that we can build the society that we are trying to build' (quoted in Hayner, 2002).

In less devious cases of affirmative repair, a semblance of the pursuit of justice is maintained, although the repair process is carefully structured to provide only superficial forms of redistribution and recognition for past injustices. In other words, material redistribution is employed to correct past injustices without seriously altering the social relations that produced these injustices, and cultural recognition is directed toward socially revaluing a specific identity or identities without challenging existing social hierarchies among competing identity groups (Fraser, 1997).[8]

These shortcomings raise the question of what 'transformative' reparations

---

7 In 1996, Mugabe, in fact, made public promises that victims of the Matabeleland atrocities would receive compensation.

8 Such is the case in British Columbia, Canada, where First Nations land claims have long gone unresolved. Upon colonising British Columbia, the colonial government failed to abide by British land occupation policy in neither conquering, nor signing treaty agreements with, the aboriginal people of this area. Moreover, subsequent claims made by the Canadian and British Columbia governments that this region was discovered as *terra nullius*, or unoccupied land, have been proven false within Canadian courts because there is much evidence of aboriginal title to the land in question (see *Calder v Attorney-General Of British Columbia*, 1973; *Delgamuukw v British Columbia*, 1997). These legal decisions forced the governments of Canada and British Columbia to join First Nations at the negotiation table to resolve this issue, but the governments' negotiation mandates have thus far proven so rigid and limiting that they provide little more than superficial redistributions of land, resources, money and political rights, rather than a broad reconfiguration of aboriginal and non-aboriginal relations in the province. After nearly 14 years in operation, the BC treaty process has produced only two treaty agreements (out of 42 tabled) because most First Nations have rejected government offers to exchange justice for 'certainty' (Ratner et al, 2003; Woolford, 2004; 2005).

might look like. Transformative repair is an ideal that often motivates victim demands, but which is seldom realised in practice. Such a practice would recognise that the crimes of the past were rooted in cultural and socio-economic relations in need of eradication so that these injustices are not repeated. Attempts to address such deep-seated injustices could neither be realised within limited timeframes (as in the case of truth commissions), nor motivated by promises of finality and certainty. Instead, conflict resolution would entail an open and developing project, unburdened by expectations of full and final closure. The effort would call for dialogue between former combatants, in which the voice of the wronged party has priority, and in which trust and mutual understanding are established over time rather than codified in fixed, contractual terms. The purpose would be to promote a mutual understanding of how social conditions contributed to the subservient position of the targeted group and how those conditions might be changed. This would require more than just the redistribution of monies and resources; efforts would need to be directed toward overhauling the structures of opportunity and wealth creation that created past injustices. Similarly, on a cultural level, transformative justice would challenge and reconfigure patterns of cultural recognition and opportunities for cultural representation within the public sphere. Ideals such as these motivated many South African activists, who hoped that the SATRC would bring about more than simply black electoral power and public recognition of suffering. As Mahmood Mamdani (2000) observed, these activists hoped for a reparations project that would remove inequalities between the *beneficiaries* and *disadvantaged* of the apartheid era, rather than merely rectify injustices committed by *perpetrators* against *victims*. Indigenous activists, as an example, often enter into reparations negotiations in pursuit of self-determination and the power to reinvigorate traditional practices, to gain increased stewardship over valuable resources and to attain cultural recognition of their 'national' status (Woolford, 2005). The scope of such reparations signifies a profound transformation of existing social relations.

Reparations within the informal–formal justice complex

The governmentality critique

Affirmative repair can be further understood in relation to the imperatives of governmentality. For example, in the aftermath of mass violence, disciplinary reparative techniques are often employed in an attempt to establish societal stability and normalise social relations. Such strategies can include enforced lessons in the 'conduct of conduct', such as the 'deNazification' policies installed by the Allies to help West Germans internalise non-fascist social values and practices (Herf, 1997). Such re-education programmes have also been implemented in post-genocide Rwanda. For example, the National Commission on Unity and Reconciliation (NCUR) runs 'solidarity camps', or *igando*, which re-educate the refugees returning to the country in addition to those assigned to the programme by the courts. This re-education lasts from one to three months, includes some military training and instruction on the notion of unity, and features speakers who lecture about Rwandan history and politics from a Rwandan Patriotic Front (RPF) perspective. These camps are now mandatory for anyone wishing to enrol in university or seeking government or military employment (Longman, 2004).

As these cases illustrate, post-conflict societies frequently enlist a cadre of actors, such as therapists and education professionals, to change citizen behaviours as a step toward healing social rifts and repairing the past. In many cases, the citizenry has been subjected to prolonged propaganda and ideological indoctrination by an authoritarian regime. No longer beholden to that regime, they are ripe for the application of disciplinary techniques that instil new modes of governance. Thus, in the Rwandan case, individuals are not simply subject to a critique of genocidaire ideology; they are also invested with a government-designed historical narrative that preaches the necessity of political unity (now under RPF rule).

Affirmative repair is also sought through *technologies of self* that encourage victims and perpetrators of mass violence to internalise notions such as 'forgiveness' and 'reconciliation' when reflecting on past harms, rather than to engage in the socially harmful discourses and practices of 'retribution' and 'revenge'. This was the modus vivendi of the South African Truth and Reconciliation Commission, which, rather than encourage participants to vent their bitter feelings toward apartheid crimes, urged conciliation and forgiveness (Acorn, 2004; Stanley, 2005). In a similar vein, Hacking refers to the governance of the 'soul' as 'a way of internalising the social order, of putting into myself those very virtues and cruelties that enable my society to survive' (1996, p 73). In the case of truth commissions, however, it is not only the individual soul, but rather the soul of the nation on which governance operates, encouraging fractious groups to accept peaceable collective identities that enable societal stability. Thus, when Bishop Desmond Tutu (2000) emphasised the notion of *ubuntu* (that is, that a person is a person through other people) as a foundational concept for the SATRC, he might be said to have advanced a technology of self that contributed to the construction of a collective South African identity, built upon a conciliatory and forgiving stance toward the past.

Under this reading, reparations politics is not simply a ruse for solidifying state control; rather, it represents an effort to enlist citizens in post-mass violence 'identification projects' (Rose, 1999, p 177), through which they might remake themselves as political subjects who share a common ethical community. In this sense, reparations politics does not operate by bringing individuals under oppressive state controls that direct their behaviour; instead, it facilitates social stability by encouraging individuals to evaluate and reconstruct their own behaviours. It achieves this task by offering formerly conflicting parties new forms of allegiance (to a collective, multi-ethnic community), systems of values (based on ethical precepts such as *ubuntu*) and modes of expression (through participatory and democratic institutions such as truth commissions). Thus, by actively engaging them in the project of choosing these markers of 'reconciliation', technologies of self serve to unite these former antagonists under a common governmentality.

Along these lines, Shearing and Kempa (2004) suggest that the 'hope' promised by reparative actions can also operate as a mode of governance. In particular, they argue that, in trying to draw hopeful lessons from the past, memorial museums can serve as sites for the promotion of specific forms of conduct. Referring to Robben Island, the apartheid prison in which inmates such as Nelson Mandela valiantly struggled to produce an educated and empowered prison community, Shearing and Kempa note that:

> Like most museums, Robben Island is a site for the preservation and exhibition of objects thought to be of lasting value. But as a site designed to promote a hope sensibility, it is also more than that. It belongs to a class that we might think of as 'governance museums'—that is, museums that are concerned with promoting sensibilities rather than with simply exhibiting valued objects.
>
> (2004, p 65)

The Robben Island prison is now a space for individual and social reinvention. Counterpoised to the efforts of inmates to educate themselves and resist, one might therefore be inspired to examine critically his or her own capacity for knowledge and empowerment.

Here, Shearing and Kempa note the critical potential of this technology of self. The commemorative space of Robben Island does not simply serve to responsibilise visitors and to set them to the task of self-policing; instead, it demands reflexivity by asking them to examine barriers to their own empowerment.

In this sense, technologies of self do not necessarily prime the subject for submission to governance; when practised with a degree of critical autonomy, they can open an individual to a practice of self that minimises the effects of domination. With regard to reparations politics, critical technologies of self may be possible through the activation of what Foucault (1977) calls 'counter-memory', which refers to those voices unheard within official representations of the past. It is precisely through broadcasting these unheard voices that actors can forge alternative conceptions of the past and come to the realisation that the resultant state of affairs is neither natural nor inevitable. Thus, counter-memory may help to incite actors to challenge and disrupt the status quo, treating it as a non-reified and historically contingent outcome.

Official representations, on the other hand, typically reinforce hegemonic social relations and, in so doing, cast alternative tellings of history as inaccurate or inconsequential, specifically those interpretations that make up the store of counter-memory that have been subordinated to dominant history (Misztal, 2004, p 77). Given the tendency of dominant history to disregard counter-memory, the opportunity to have counter-memories heard and acknowledged within reparative settings put in motion the visionary promise of reparations politics. Such reparative encounters, however, cannot afford to foreclose discussion by establishing an alternative, but equally rigid, 'counter-truth', lest they become a mirror image of the official history that they seek to replace. The goal is to strive for what Cohen refers to as:

> Social truth: the truth generated by interaction, discussion and debate. [Truth commission] hearings provide transparency and encourage participation. Conflicting views about the past can be considered and compared. It is the process that matters, rather than the end result.
>
> (2001, p 228)

In sum, open-ended reparative encounters nurture a critical technology of self, by disrupting dominant narratives of history and by enabling new and empowered self-understandings to arise based upon alternative tellings of the past.

Communicative action and reparations

Habermas has similarly highlighted the importance of opening the discussion of history to multiple voices. As a German philosopher, Habermas has been an active participant in that nation's attempts to deal with a sullied past. In particular, Habermas was a key figure in what has come to be known as the *Historikerstreit* (or historians') debate that erupted in post-Holocaust Germany over questions of how to know and remember the Nazi past (see Maier, 1988; Pensky, 1989). The debate largely revolved around the issues of whether or not Nazi atrocities were unique and whether or not German nationhood could ever recover from the stigma of these events (Maier, 1988). In his intervention, Habermas argued that contemporary Germans had inherited from their forebears a 'form of life' that had made genocide and mass violence possible: 'The simple fact is that even those born later have grown up in a context of life [Lebensform] in which *that* was possible' (quoted in Maier, 1988, p 57). Based on this inheritance, Habermas, borrowing and reworking the notion of Walter Benjamin (1969) of 'anamnestic solidarity', counselled that contemporary Germans are forbidden from 'an unreflective and facile reappropriation of cultural traditions' (Pensky, 1989, p 357).

Can one claim to be the legal heir of the German Reich, can one continue the traditions of German culture, without taking historical responsibility for the form of life in which Auschwitz was possible? Can one take responsibility for the interconnected origins of those crimes with which our own existence is historically woven in any other way than by means of a solidaristic memory of what is now irreparable, in any other way than by means of a reflective, critical attitude vis-à-vis the traditions that endow our identity?

(Habermas, quoted in Maier, 1988, p 59)

In this way, Habermas employs his notion of the lifeworld, or 'form of life', to draw attention to the fact that an unsavoury heritage is sometimes preserved within the lifeworld's communicative space. Communicative action, thus, must be directed toward rooting out those elements of collective existence that have permitted tragedies such as Auschwitz to occur. In this sense, communicative action and discourse ethics take on a reparative role by enabling societies to address past crimes and to reconstruct a collective identity that is less susceptible to such destructive behaviours.

Elsewhere, Habermas (1994) argues that communal or national solidarity should not be built upon a blinkered and unquestioning attitude toward one's country. In other words, we owe no blind obedience to our national 'form of life', nor are we expected to silence all criticism of national failings and transgressions. Instead, he proposes that citizens adhere to a 'constitutional patriotism', whereby their allegiances are directed toward democratic practices and values. Under this conception, plurality, dissent and debate, and the institutions and rights that enable them, are vital components of a democratic order and are worthy of our loyalty. According to Nagy (2002, p 329), the South African Truth and Reconciliation Commission contributed to this type of solidarity building with the establishment of an institutional framework through which victims could contest dominant historical narratives and have their experiences publicly acknowledged. Thus, South Africa was able to build unity through the practice of reparative deliberation, rather than by clinging to or constructing anew a mythological national identity.

Indeed, it is the deliberative potential of reparations politics that many authors find most promising. Alan Cairns (2003, p 83) sees reparations as a part of 'democratising the past', through which a democratic sense of equal recognition is given to those who have been marginalised and victimised. For him, reparations means challenging 'official' history so that other narratives can emerge and garner public acceptance. Likewise, Barkan (2000; 2003) sees in reparations politics a greater willingness on the part of democracies to open their pasts to discursive engagement through processes of national self-reflection. For him, these processes represent the 'new guilt of nations' (2003, p 92) and are opportunities for public engagement on the question of national identity. Maier (2003, p 297), likewise, describes reparations as removing 'losses from the realm of the sacred, the never-to-be-forgiven, into the realm of the politically negotiated'. This allows communication to resume between adversaries and creates possibilities for 'political reconciliation' (2003, p 298), defined by a return to political, cultural and commercial interaction.

Reflecting on demands made by descendants of slaves in the USA, Thomas McCarthy draws a similar conclusion:

> ... [T]he reparations movement could ignite a public debate in our mass-mediated public sphere and ... this could eventually prove of great 'public-pedagogical' significance in raising and reforming public historical consciousness. The structured forms provided by public trials, public hearings, commissions of inquiry, and the like are settings in which the massive gap between professional historiography and public memory might be narrowed somewhat; that is to say, in which the dismal state of public awareness of the actual history of slavery and segregation in the United States, of the extent to which it has shaped our culture and institutions, and of the pervasive structural inequalities it has left behind could be improved.
>
> (2004, p 765)

Thus, for McCarthy, it is this 'public-pedagogical' element of reparations politics, a phrase he borrows from Laura Hein (2003), which holds the greatest potential for shifting public memory toward an honest reckoning with the past. In this sense, it is not so much monetary or resource redistribution that is most significant about reparations politics; rather, it is the opportunity for democratic deliberation over reparations that is most promising (McCarthy, 2004, pp 766–7).

Underlying these perspectives on the democratic potential of reparative deliberations are the presuppositions of discourse ethics. Reparative events, like truth commissions, ideally assume that all parties have an equal chance to speak and be heard (whether through public testimony or published interviews), that they can raise whatever issues they deem important and that they can do so in an environment that is free of coercion. In the context of reparations talks, this 'ideal speech situation' is obviously conducive to respectful dialogue about the past and can have salutary impact on broader reparations policy.

The prospects for reparations in the informal–formal justice complex

It must be recognised, however, that the various forms of reparations politics may prove difficult spaces for the creation of critical technologies of self, or for meeting the presuppositions of discourse ethics, if they are too infused with dominant political and legal rationalities, and if their outcomes are prefigured by the restrictive demands of affirmative repair. These pressures limit the transformative potential of reparations politics by harnessing reparations to prevalent modes of juridical and neoliberal thought, preventing adoption of a truly critical and disruptive stance in relation to the past. Thus, despite the fact that many reparative practices exhibit informal characteristics that make them technically distinct from tribunals and other formal legal responses to past injustices, they are nonetheless entrenched within the informal–formal justice complex: that is, they sit in a complementary relationship with formal legal and political systems, and function to support and stabilise, rather than to disrupt, these systems.

Precisely because reparations politics may reinforce dominant power relations, in order to assess the transformative potential of reparations politics, we must once again consider how various forms of reparations are subject to the three levels of power discussed in the previous chapters on mediation and restorative justice:

- broader systems of power;
- power relations within the juridical field;
- power relations within the subfield of reparations politics.

Under the influence of these pressures, the tendency is toward reparative governmentalities that affirm dominant social relations.

First, in respect of broader systems of power, neoliberal policies and globalisation dynamics have undoubtedly had an impact on reparations politics. Under neoliberal conditions, affirmative strategies of repair have become common means by which to encourage reparative practices that are consonant with the demands of contemporary governance. Within a globalising system of nation states, under which competition exists to lure the investment and industry of a mobile capital, countries have an interest in promoting societal stability and minimising conflict. While many nations employ heavy-handed and oppressive strategies to create the appearance of stability, others exploit reparations politics as a way to minimise public discontent and to foster a welcoming investment climate. For neoliberal regimes following this strategy, reparative practices are viewed as a relatively efficient means for effecting a societal transition through which governable social relations can be established, provided the claimant group is willing to exchange their broader demands for a limited settlement package. By investing in the cathartic power of truth commissions, public commemoration, apology and compensation, these regimes strive to reconstitute the nation as a secure economic and political arena.

As an example, reparations processes designed to deal with the justice demands of indigenous peoples often represent tactical attempts to overcome the disruptive nature of these groups. Their claimed status as nations within nations, and their demands for self-determination and recognition of a culturally distinct mode of life, threaten dominant notions of nationhood and, in some cases, dominant modes of economic production (for example, if claims of environmental stewardship conflict with resource extraction activities). Rather than fully acknowledge these claims through nation-to-nation negotiation processes, it is not uncommon for (neo-)colonial governments to make reparations offers designed to integrate indigenous peoples into national, cultural and economic patterns by granting them a financial stake in resource extraction industries, or by installing them in government or justice positions so that, ironically, they might strengthen local governance. In this manner, reparations can be directed toward a responsibilisation strategy through negotiations that offer immediate perks to indigenous peoples in exchange for the secession of their socially destabilising justice demands. As an example, the Howard government in Australia has refused to participate in reparative processes that take a 'black armband' approach to history, by which it means reconciliation efforts predicated upon settler atonement for the injustices caused to Australian Aboriginal peoples. Instead, it has pursued what it terms 'practical reconciliation', which involves, among other things, an increasing tendency to treat Aboriginal people as 'market individuals who choose their strategies for education, employment, political representation and domestic culture from among the options available' (Austin-Broos, 2004, p 309).

Second, in respect of power relations within the juridical field, the informal–formal justice complex asserts its influence on reparations politics through the increased presence of juridical rationalities within human rights discourses and justice practices.

The establishment of a legal edifice for enforcing human rights and international justice has been a hard-fought battle. The United Nations Convention on the Prevention and Punishment of Genocide, the Universal Declaration of Human Rights and the Rome Statute of the International Criminal Court, to name but a few prominent examples, have all been viewed as threats to sovereignty by specific powerful states. Thus, it is difficult to view their existence as anything but a humanitarian achievement. Nonetheless, they are also reflective of a juridical mode of thinking about justice that brings to international politics the rationalities of the Western legal field. As laws, they designate a privileged caste of actors (that is, lawyers and judges) as their interpreters. In addition, the harms they identify are understood as 'crimes', which therefore locates them within a legal value system that presumes that such crimes will be met with an appropriate judicial response.

Most reparations claims are made based upon such international legal codes; thus, the juridical field serves as the foundation for much reparations politics, and therefore rituals of negotiation and public atonement, even if taking place outside of the courtroom, have law at their root. Moreover, these reparative rituals are increasingly subject to legal standards, which may have a detrimental effect on their communicative goals. As Christodoulidis (2000) observes, reconciliation requires a degree of open-endedness, so that individuals can tell their stories of perpetration and abuse free from artificially imposed limitations; truth commissions such as the SATRC often impose such limitations through their embrace of legal interpretations and formulations.

> In every aspect of its working, the TRC was steeped in law; it engaged in legal interpretations of key notions—'just ends, just means' and 'crime against humanity'; 'victim'; 'severe ill-treatment'; 'political context, political motivation'; 'accountability'. It enjoyed significant procedural powers, among them, the power to issue subpoenas and force people before it, to compel witnesses' testimony; to decide on the admissibility of evidence; to authorise searches and seizures; to subpoena documents; to grant amnesties.
>
> (2000, p 187)

As such, truth commissions often remain firmly entrenched within the informal–formal justice complex, resulting in the imposition of formal juridical scripts upon these allegedly informal interactions. These scripts narrow the possibilities for critical engagement because they insist on reductive distillations of complicated historical events. For example, they require clear designations of 'victim' and 'perpetrator', even though these identities can sometimes be muddled and confused in cases of mass violence (Mamdani, 2001). Such simplifications distort and trivialise the aims of communicative deliberation, because they place limits on what can be spoken and how it might be said.

Other forms of reparations politics are similarly entrenched within the informal–formal justice complex and thus also the juridical field. For example, negotiations for compensation are typically carried out either in the shadow of the formal justice system, in the sense that the monetary amount potentially obtainable through a lawsuit might serve as a basis for the agreed-upon compensation amount, or within the courts, such as the lawsuit filed by Deadria Farmer-Paellmann in the US District Court for the Eastern District of New York for compensation from corporations that profited from African American slavery (Torpey, 2006). Symbolic reparations, such as apologies and statements of regret, are also often carefully worded so that they will not be construed as an admission of responsibility within a court of law and thereby result in unwanted liability. In these and other cases, the insertion of such informal justice practices within the informal–formal justice complex restricts their transformative potential by encouraging strategic interventions that operate in accordance with a juridical and instrumental rationality. Thus, the increasing influence of juridical practices on reparations politics is more than just a problem of professionalisation and the loss of informal control of justice processes; it represents a narrowing of the communicative space available for assailing and disrupting unjust social conditions.

Third, in respect of power relations within the practice of reparations politics, international negotiators and facilitators have, in many cases, bracketed progressive or transformative objectives, resigning themselves to strategies that are consistent with prevailing juridical notions, and the reigning rationalities of neoliberalism and globalisation. In general, they lean toward either 'power-political' models of negotiation, which emphasise bargaining, leverage and compromise among other tools for bringing about a speedy settlement, or 'facilitative' ones, which seek to establish problem-solving communication between combatants through the interventions of a neutral negotiator (Jones, 2000). In both cases, however, the tendency is toward affirmative resolutions. In the former, political suasion is blatantly employed and advantages the stronger party in achieving favourable settlements. In the latter, although facilitation seeks to strike a balanced discussion between combatants, it is rare that conflicting parties are equal in their possession of power and the stronger party often seeks to win the negotiation. Under such conditions, it is extremely difficult for reparations processes to break free from dominant logics of governance, because the victimised parties rarely stand on the same footing with their former victimisers and are seldom able to determine the outcome of negotiations. Moreover, as negotiators and mediators are often culled from the worlds of politics and international law, they tend to be versed in the rationality of realpolitik, and are inclined to prioritise peace and stability 'on the ground' over a seemingly abstract ideal of justice (Doubt, 2000).

With these and other limitations in place, power relations within the practice of reparations politics gravitate toward juridical and instrumental settlements rather than transformative goals. Victim groups, the non-governmental organisations that support them and their lawyers are often fully aware of what is attainable under these economic and political constraints, and will thus opt to pursue whatever limited recompense is available given these circumstances. Reparations lawsuits directed against corporations and governments, therefore, might seem a more promising path to remediation than the chimera of broader societal transformations that might offer the victim group a stronger sense of inclusion and opportunity within the dominant society. Then, too, victim groups may view such legal challenges as the most promising initial steps toward the pursuit of transformative justice, assuming that they direct the minimal resources and recognition provided through affirmative repair toward building a more powerful movement for social change. In the words of George Dor, former general secretary of Jubilee South Africa, an organisation promoting debt relief:

> For us, the [reparations claims-making] is just one way of maintaining momentum. For us, it's a social movement leading the legal cases, not the other way around. Individual reparations are legally most important, but politically they're least important. Monetary reparations

are not irrelevant, but they're only a catalyst for broader social transformation.

(Dor, quoted in Torpey, 2006, p 150)

Consequently, even though all three levels of power seem designed to impose a narrow affirmative script on reparations politics, it is nevertheless evident that reparations politics is not entirely bereft of opportunities for empowerment. Within truth commissions, reparations negotiations and communicative history, critical discourses and counter-memories can emerge to interrogate patterns of domination. A public truth commission can create broader awareness of the injustices perpetrated under a previous regime and lead to reflection on the social conditions that made it possible for this situation to arise. Reparations payments can signify that a state truly recognises the legitimacy of victim justice claims and deems them worthy of state investment, thereby promoting wider acceptance and acknowledgement of victims. And a commemorative museum might provoke consideration of not only a single tragic event, such as the Holocaust, but also of current world problems, such as the genocide in Darfur. These reparative processes, whatever their substantive outcomes, can initiate deliberative engagements that might enable individuals to think more clearly about the factors that propel incidents of mass violence and collective injustice.

The difficulty, once again, is in directing these deliberative insights toward political change and it is here that the three levels of power discussed above are most salient. Empowering moments of insight and discovery quickly come up against barriers that dilute their potential impact. Neoliberal governments are likely to ignore those truth commission recommendations that are deemed impractical under prevailing economic rationalities, such as SATRC suggestions that a 'wealth tax' be administered in South Africa to redistribute funds from the rich to the poor. Likewise, once the initial excitement of entering reparations negotiations with a new (or newly repentant) government dies down, a victims' group may find itself faced with the decision of whether to accept an expedient offer or to persist in its broader justice demands. A 'reality check' from its legal counsel or mediator may persuade the group to accept the offer, although this will likely bring to an end public discussion of its outstanding claims. Moreover, subsequent attempts to sustain those claims by using funds gained through affirmative repair may no longer attract a once-supportive public that assumes a settlement has occurred. For victim movements, new strategies and institutional channels to arouse public memory and foster deliberation on the injustices they experienced become requisite. This brings us to the subject of our final chapter: how might informal justice practices be redirected toward achieving transformative ends?

Conclusion

In this chapter, we have:

- described the informal field of reparations politics as consisting of truth commissions, compensation, symbolic politics, restitution and communicative history;
- outlined the historical development of reparations politics. Initially, reparations were solely the right of states, but through the efforts of victim movements—namely, the Jewish organisations that sought indemnification from West Germany for crimes committed during World War II—reparations became a demand made by survivors of mass violence;
- discussed claims that reparations politics lacks a progressive vision, and has become increasingly professionalised and juridified;
- articulated an ideal-type distinction between 'affirmative' and 'transformative' reparations to capture a key contrast between the political goals of various reparations processes;
- positioned reparations within the informal–formal justice complex. Although reparations politics are not unhindered by state involvement, they do offer a space for public deliberation on important historical events. In this manner, we discussed the overlap between Foucault's notion of counter-memory and Habermas' suppositions on the responsibility to take a critical attitude toward the past. Both theorists underscore the power of public discourse to challenge the dominant narratives of history and gain recognition (and redress) for past injustices;
- noted the several barriers that block disruptive insights from fostering political change. Both the neoliberal logics of rule that govern many contemporary nations and the dominant forms of juridical reasoning that guide reparations politics impel governments and negotiators to pursue 'affirmative' forms of repair, leaving transformative insights with little political traction.

Chapter 6

Informal justice counterpublics

We have argued throughout these chapters that the informal–formal justice complex routinely combines seemingly contradictory informal and formal justice practices. In so doing, it enables the maintenance and reproduction of a juridical field that privileges the interventions of legal professionals and extends the reach of neoliberal governmentality by enlisting informal empowerment to the task of individual responsibilisation. In this manner, informal practices intended to promote creative deliberations on issues of public interest become scripted and diluted, lessening their potential to envision transformative change.

The prospects for disrupting the informal–formal justice complex

In the preceding chapters, we have identified civil mediation, restorative justice and reparations politics as key moments in the reparative turn. Roughly around the 1970s, these three types of 'informal justice' gained momentum and inspired the hope that justice might be conducted through the active participation of everyday people, rather than by the interventions of professional practitioners or the state. This democratic approach to justice, it was held, would engender ideas and resolutions designed to address specific harms and to repair resultant individual and collective needs. Individuals would be empowered to relate their narratives of suffering and wrongdoing, and informal processes would allow for contextually specific responses to these harms. These informal processes would derive their legitimacy not from the state, but from the consensual agreement of the key stakeholders—those directly affected by or complicit in the wrongful act(s).

This vision of justice, however, came up against the perplexing reality of the informal–formal justice complex. Informal justice could not find for itself an independent space, free from the dictates and rationalities of formal justice systems. Necessarily tied to formal justice, the ideal of informal justice gave way to more restricted and circumscribed models that offered only temporary and fleeting forms of empowerment.

Civil mediation, in the form of community justice, possessed perhaps the greatest potential for autonomy from formal justice, because it could, at least theoretically, draw on local actors and resources to conduct its operations. If referrals came from community members, rather than from state gatekeepers, and if local funding was used to support community justice operations, informal justice could potentially sever practical ties with formal administrative systems. But this separation from formal justice was, in actuality, very difficult to achieve and few, if any, community mediation programmes succeeded in this regard. For this reason, those sceptical of informal justice saw community mediation as an extension, rather than a withdrawal, of state power. Governmentality scholars added further doubts by noting the ways in which community mediation programmes induced participants to become active agents in forms of self-governance that rendered them docile subjects. They saw the governing logic of neoliberalism at play within community mediation, encouraging conflict resolution with minimal taxation of state resources, a frugal tendency that was reinforced by increasing juridical incursions into civil mediation as a means of hastening justice delivery. More and more lawyers thus lay claim to mediation as a component of their conflict resolution toolkit and compete openly with non-professional mediators for clients. In response, non-lawyer mediators, seeking to professionalise their practice and ensure a steady clientele, attach their services to formal legal channels. As a result of these developments, the overall practice of mediation has become further entrenched within the informal–formal justice complex, making it more difficult to pursue, much less imagine, a transformative course.

Unlike mediation, contemporary restorative justice is integrally connected to the formal justice system. Predicated on 'crime', restorative justice practitioners take officially sanctioned 'law' as their starting point. Thus, in order to access criminal cases, they most often rely upon the courts to divert cases to restorative justice programmes. This presents dangers of co-optation as well as concerns that restorative justice will be used strategically to target, for example, minor and youth crimes, thereby widening the net of state control. Moreover, as governmentality studies scholars have warned, the reputedly empowering deliberative practices of restorative justice can be harnessed to the orthodox rationalities of criminal justice, especially when restorative justice programmes are prevented from addressing harms not defined as 'crime', as well as harms caused by the application of unjust laws (Pavlich, 2005). Clearly, the effects of restorative justice programmes, now proliferating in neoliberal regimes and purportedly aimed at devolving criminal justice responsibilities to communities and individuals, are blunted by the involvement of criminal justice professionals within the everyday practice of restorative justice. Police officers, lawyers and judges have become necessary players in most restorative justice programmes, acting as gatekeepers, administrators and facilitators of their operations. With them, they bring the dominant rationalities of criminal justice. Moreover, as government and even non-government funders (for example, United Way) insist on 'outcome'- or 'results'-oriented services, restorative justice agencies—competing for funds and referrals—are compelled to shape their programmes in line with market objectives. Thus, a confluence of extrinsic factors limits, and degrades, the communicative and transformative potential of this mode of informal justice.

Of the three types of informal justice discussed here, reparations politics is perhaps most squarely situated within the informal–formal justice complex. The state, both as a perpetrator of injustices and as a facilitator of justice, is, in most cases, an indispensable player in reparations politics. Truth commissions, reparations, restitution, symbolic politics and communicative history all depend on state involvement and state support for their success.[1] This makes them potential vehicles for aggrandisements of state control and professional power, in that they serve to reclaim state authority and legitimacy in the aftermath of shameful events. At the same time, these reparative stratagems subtly inculcate an ethos of reconciliation that obscures the state's reassertion of power. So, while these forms of post-atrocity justice are less formal and more deliberative than are trials and tribunals, contradictory pressures undermine their transformative potential. As discussed earlier, their application in the context of neoliberal-charged demands for order tends to restrict outcomes to 'affirmative repair'. Stability, governability and economy rank more importantly than fundamental change. Indeed, the dialogue that flows out of these communicative contexts is hedged by legal concerns: what can be said without deviating from the prescribed focus and without incurring legal liability? Especially in the realm of reparations politics, in which the cost of failed conflict resolution can trigger a renewal of hostilities, negotiators are wont to prioritise realpolitik objectives, such as achieving a halt to conflict, rather than to pursue the broader demands of transformative justice.

Thus, there are many factors that diminish or thwart the potential of these three forms of informal justice, given their situs within the informal–formal justice complex. But the existence of limiting pressures does not mean that transformative and empowering opportunities cannot arise.

As we have maintained throughout, mediation, restorative justice and reparations are not united under a single philosophy or mode of practice. Within each informal justice type, there are movements directed toward a more progressive practice of justice—that is, transformative mediation, communitarian restorative justice and transformative reparations. These

---

1 A potential exception would be what is often referred to as 'public memory'—the store of popular remembrances of an historical event or trauma. Public memory includes, but is not limited to, fictional representations, media portrayals, private journals and photographs, popular song and impromptu memorials. These private commemorations both draw from, and contribute to, formal remembrances of the sort that we describe as reparations politics.

progressive strands do, in some cases, offer ways in which to minimise the effects of state power and to achieve 'limited' or 'momentary' disruptions within the informal–formal justice complex. Moreover, individual actors participating in informal justice encounters can obtain a 'feel for the game', in the sense that they realise what is practically achievable through the medium of the informal–formal justice complex, which they might accept as a temporary resolution while retaining their broader justice ideals. In other words, all political agency is not lost within the trappings of the informal–formal justice complex.

To consider a few concrete possibilities, a mediator employing the model of 'transformative mediation' suggested by Bush and Folger (1994) might assist adversaries in achieving a sense of 'empowerment' and 'recognition', and these experiences may prove disruptive in certain contexts. Such a mediator would not seek to impose solutions upon the parties in conflict, but would encourage the parties to take ownership of the conflict, to define it in their own terms and thus to increase their capacity to 'recognise' the needs and experiences of others, as well as to affirm their own ability to deal with challenging situations. For example, tenants and a landlord in a mediated conflict over substandard living conditions would be encouraged to articulate their own sensibilities with regards to the rights and needs of renters. This experience might make the landlord more aware of the everyday hardships experienced by those living in shoddy conditions; it might also strengthen the tenants' resolve to take more concerted action in demanding that their living conditions be improved. Transformative mediation, here, entails a disruption of the power relationship that exists between renters and property owners.

Likewise, restorative justice might potentially allow a community to address destructive social patterns that extend beyond a specific criminal event. Thus, circle sentencing in an aboriginal community that has experienced high rates of alcoholism, suicide, and physical and sexual abuse may allow the community to consider more deeply the impact that colonialism has had on their lives. Their embrace of healing circles may be viewed as an initial step toward reasserting the community's powers of self-determination, and the circles themselves may offer an opportunity to dissect the strategies of assimilation that have assailed its cultural traditions and institutions, including the role that criminal and other forms of law have played in colonial domination. Indeed, these broader ideals guided the healing circles that were employed in the community of Hollow Water, Manitoba, where cycles of violence and sexual abuse had engulfed the community, making most members of the community victims and/or perpetrators. The circle programme dealt not only with specific cases of abuse, but also with the loss of a sense of community empowerment, and the circles were viewed as a first step toward regaining local autonomy. Thus, although these circles were established by the Canadian government at the request of the Hollow Water First Nation and were conducted within the framework of Canadian law, they nonetheless opened a space for public reflection on the harmful consequences of Canadian colonialism.

Finally, reparations politics, even if directed toward affirmative goals, does create opportunities for at least moderate disruptions of social domination. For instance, reparative events emanating from post-Nazi Germany and post-Apartheid South Africa, as well as continuing efforts to achieve repair in places such as Sierra Leone, Nigeria and Burma, have raised questions about the responsibilities of corporations to abide by human rights standards and to withdraw financial support from regimes that mistreat their citizens. Although, in some cases, the accused corporations have successfully fought off the charges, a dialogue has been established and citizen-led pressure has been placed on oil companies, arms manufacturers and the purveyors of 'blood diamonds', to name but a few, to recognise the human consequences of their economic practices.

Progressive achievements such as these are not to be dismissed. Although they are often only momentary and relations of power are quickly readjusted so as to resolve their threat, their effects can accumulate and inspire broader social change. The challenge lies in multiplying these limited disruptions so that they have sustained effect. Bush and Folger's (1994) notion that individual change inspired through transformative mediation can spread through societal relations and thereby provoke broader social change, can only be realised if these transformative moments can be somehow aggregated and given political direction. And this is a difficult challenge given the prevalence of systemic constraints, which are also cumulative in their effect because they operate at multiple levels to dilute and compromise informal moments of empowerment and critical engagement.

It is here that governmentality studies' criticisms are most salient. One reason that these attempts at transformative justice are so difficult to sustain is that these disruptive moments are rendered inert when they are reshaped into order-maintaining technologies of self and techniques of discipline. Rather than sparking a continuous critical struggle that deeply probes the causes and sources of social injustice, informal justice empowerment tends to encourage subjects who foreswear and/or minimise conflict. In cases in which social injustices are entrenched and persistent, such conciliatory behaviour is often inopportune, halting radical engagements before they can generate social change.

This brings us to the question of whether there might be a means to invigorate informal justice, so that it might more easily spark 'radical disruptions' that amplify and extend the potential for transformative justice. These disruptions would transgress conventional justice boundaries, defy the tenets and precepts of neoliberal governance, and yield tangible political effects. In this manner, they would move beyond a narrowly defined range of possibilities for change, toward broader assaults on the juridical power undergirding unjust social relations.

But what is the space from which such radical disruptions can be launched? Is it possible to reconfigure current practices of informal justice and to initiate a transformative justice politics from within the informal–formal justice complex? Or would it be necessary to retreat to a space outside the informal–formal justice complex, ideally beyond its hegemonic reach? Several options may be proposed for locating the staging point of transformative justice, each with its own set of strategic advantages and disadvantages.

First, an attempt might be made to situate conflict resolution practices outside of the informal–formal justice complex. This would be much like the role Melucci (1987; 1994; 1995) envisions for 'nomadic' new social movements. By remaining on the margins of the political, Melucci suggests that new social movements can articulate the injustices experienced in the everyday lives of individuals and call for their remedy without needing to accept institutionalisation or co-optation as means by which to achieve political recognition. Thus, social movements become exterior spaces for the articulation and practice of alternative modes of thought and action. Similarly, informal conflict resolution experiments might be established on the margins of society, away from the influence of law and government, so that they might enhance citizen empowerment and creativity. For example, a group of like-minded individuals possessing land and resources might form a retreatist community in which all conflicts are dealt with informally, with no recourse to state actors. Less radically, a community justice programme might attempt to operate free of state referrals and funding, relying instead on local resources. Under such conditions, the community could achieve sufficient independence and capacity to conceive and implement alternatives to dominant juridical practices. Such attempts fail, however, to provide any clear guidance as to how marginal public spaces can be expanded to spread the concerns of the movement to a broader audience (Bartholomew and Mayer, 1992; Scott, 1990). The inviolability of the extra-institutional space envisioned seems little more than a recipe for the permanent marginalisation and trivialisation of informal challengers to dominant juridical codes. Moreover, with specific reference to reparations politics, such separation is not realistic, because the state, as mentioned above, is usually a necessary participant in these informal processes.

Second, informal conflict resolution might continue to operate within the informal–formal justice complex with the aim of transforming it from within—on the assumption that multiple trials would eventually overhaul the justice system. This strategy currently guides the efforts of many informal justice practitioners, who envision their institutionalised civil mediation, restorative justice or truth commission programmes as modelling a different approach to justice. These practitioners assume that, as the public becomes more aware of the benefits of these informal justice models, they will become more convinced of the effectiveness and fairness of non-adversarial justice. This outcome, however, rests on a questionable premise: that the practice of informal justice is sufficiently compelling as to gradually shift justice discourse in a more progressive direction. Unfortunately, to date, the history of informal justice practices indicates that they are more likely to be absorbed within the informal–formal justice complex and utilised to enhance affirmative modes of domination.

Third, and differing slightly from the above, an attempt might be made to carve out a space for distinct informal justice values *within* the informal–formal justice complex. Indeed, this approach is a familiar one among informal justice practitioners, who go about their business within the criminal justice system while trying to enact and gain support for more progressive approaches from other justice professionals. This requires that informal justice proponents enunciate and uphold their values (Zehr, 1995) or, colloquially speaking, 'walk the talk' (Van Ness and Heetderks Strong, 1997). In this vein, proponents of civil mediation, restorative justice and reparations politics emphasise values such as non-coercive communication, participant empowerment and a holistic approach to healing harm. These values then serve as a touchstone in situations within which compromising or co-opting pressures are placed upon informal justice programmes. For example, when confronted by a state demand that they meet a certain caseload quota and restrict facilitated encounters to two-hour sessions, a restorative justice or mediation agency would ignore such dictates and adhere to the principle that conflict resolution must unfold at whatever pace allows for maximum healing. The allure of this principled approach is that the agency remains engaged with justice institutions, rather than hived off in a marginal space, while also defending itself against state co-optation. The drawback is that, because it remains in a defensive posture, much of its energy is directed toward protecting informal justice programmes against state- and professional-led incursions. In this sense, the approach lacks a coherent long-term strategy for instigating systemic change. Moreover, the sedulous efforts to *preserve* restorative justice values detract from the need for informal justice programmes to reflect critically on these values so that they they might, for example, recognise the extent to which their value systems are predicated on, and infused with, neoliberal and juridical forms of reasoning.

One more option to be considered is that which requires informal justice exponents to oscillate between engagement in and withdrawal from the informal–formal justice complex. The envisioned space of withdrawal serves as an arena for value creation and critical disruption of dominant social codes, and also as a political space in which tactical interventions against the informal–formal justice complex can be conceived and then undertaken. It is this potentially fruitful, if risky, option, to which we assign the label 'informal justice counterpublics' that we now turn. It should be noted at the outset, however, that informal justice counterpublics are an analytical ideal rather than a present reality. The characteristics described below are aspirational, in the sense that they provide a guide for transformation-minded informal justice programmes. Examples will be provided of organisations that, in our estimation, seek to become informal justice counterpublics.

Becoming informal justice counterpublics

The informal justice movement has frequently located itself within the 'community', imagining this as a non-coercive space in which like-minded people can support and encourage one another. As critics have pointed out, however, community is, in fact, a notion built upon social exclusion (Pavlich, 2001). To be part of a community is to assume that there are others who are *not* part of this social unit. What is meant by 'community' is something synonymous with mutual understanding, homogeneity and shared beliefs. For these reasons, community is an inappropriate location for transformative informal justice, because the critical self-reflection that threatens to counter the taken-for-granted precepts of community life is often discouraged (Bauman, 2001). In search of a more emancipatory space for informal justice, one might instead locate informal justice in the 'public', a space of collective reflection and deliberation in which dearly held principles might be subjected to debate and critically interrogated (Strang and Braithwaite, 2001). It must be acknowledged, however, that traditional notions of the public have also been built upon social exclusion: in Greece, slaves, women and foreigners were excluded from public deliberation; in other traditions, property ownership was a requisite for public engagement (Angus, 2001, p 42).

Habermas has sought a reconstructed notion of the public sphere grounded in the principles of communicative action and discourse ethics—but, even operating on Habermas' presuppositions of non-coercion and rationality, this form of public sphere is not free from moments of domination and exclusion. First, Habermas overlooks those subtle forms of manipulation and control that are encoded into the conventions of discourse. While Habermas recommends that differences in status be bracketed upon entry into the public sphere, this bracketing is likely only to mask and mystify prevailing inequalities (Fraser, 1992). Status inequalities are embedded within practices of communication, lending those with higher status a greater degree of 'cultural capital' (Bourdieu, 1991), and allowing them to appear more at ease, natural and competent within their communicative milieux. Pretending that these differentials do not exist prevents questions from being raised within the public sphere about these practice-based inequalities.

Second, Habermas assumes the existence of a unitary and comprehensive public sphere comprised of the totality of public interactions. While such a public sphere allows for democratic participation in a project toward establishing the common good, Fraser (1992) notes that there is also valuable democratic benefit to be gained from the multiplication of micro-public spheres that attend to particularistic concerns. Fraser (1997, p 81) terms these 'subaltern counterpublics', which 'are parallel discursive arenas where members of subordinated social groups invent and circulate counterdiscourses, which in turn permit them to formulate oppositional interpretations of their identities, interests and needs'. In this manner, these counterpublics serve as checks against the tendency of the public sphere to reproduce the dominant social order. As Fraser suggests:

> On the one hand, they function as spaces of withdrawal and regroupment; on the other hand, they also function as bases and training grounds for agitational activities directed toward wider publics. It is precisely in the dialectic between these two functions that their emancipatory potential lies.
>
> (1997, p 82)

It is also here that the transformative potential of informal justice lies. The mistake made too frequently is to locate informal justice within a space that is already integrated within prevailing systems of power and inundated with a juridical ethos that stifles its creative potential. A uniquely experimental space is required that allows for alternative modalities to be conceived and practised. In the pursuit of this objective, the notion of the counterpublic is a useful ideal:

> The goals of these counterpublics include understanding themselves better, forging bonds of solidarity, preserving the memories of past injustices, interpreting and reinterpreting the meanings of those injustices, working out alternative conceptions of self, of community, of justice, and of universality, trying to make sense of both the privileges they wield and the oppressions they face, understanding the strategic configurations for and against their desired ends, deciding what alliances to make both emotionally and strategically, deliberating on ends and means, and deciding how to act both individually and collectively.
>
> (Mansbridge, 1996, p 58)

Likewise, informal justice counterpublics ideally foster reflection upon the practices of justice, interpretations of injustice, the identities produced through injustice and administrations of justice, the social and political values upheld and forwarded through justice practices, and the means and ends of justice. But these critical functions are lost when such counterpublics are woven into the fabric of the informal–formal justice complex. Informal justice counterpublics need to operate in a space from which they can challenge the grammar of justice, rethinking the codes and traditions that hold sway over everyday justice practices, including those forwarded by informal justice proponents.

By offering opportunities for actors to challenge reigning juridical and neoliberal norms, informal justice counterpublics also create space for the formation of new justice identities. Orville Lee, building on Fraser's notion, states that:

> Counterpublics can also be organised as sites for symbolic experimentation in which social identities and categories are de- and re-constructed. They are social spaces in which class, sexual, racial and gender hybridity and transgressions of ascribed socio-cultural identities are practiced. This type of counterpublic is the hothouse of a transformative politics of culture.
>
> (1998, p 449)

Lee's description suggests that the inclusion in informal justice counterpublics of those who are marginalised from formal justice systems—those who commit, contribute to or suffer various forms of social harm—opens these public arenas to new discursive potentials. Informal justice counterpublics, therefore, would not simply reproduce the identities and dispositions of prefigured justice actors (for example, victim, offender and innocent bystander); rather, they would offer staging grounds for the development of an alternative culture of justice in which people could be understood as simultaneously harmed and harming, so that a broader range of forms of social suffering and solutions might be considered.

Informal justice counterpublics, however, need to aspire to be more than reclusive zones within which the boundaries of the informal–formal justice complex are called into question. They must also function as the seedbeds for oppositional activities that can alter patterns of political decision-making and economic inequality. As previously noted, governmentality studies (à la Foucault) underline the necessity of disrupting diffuse and pervasive rationalities of power in order to prevent the sedimentation of unchallenged logics of governance and domination. Discourse ethics (à la Habermas) theorise the ideal dialogical space in which critical engagements might take place, rippling out to broader arenas of policy deliberation. To mirror these fundamental conditions, informal justice counterpublics must, at bottom:

- examine the obstacles to transformative change represented by juridical and neoliberal logics;
- persevere as critical and reflexive agents bent on resisting modes of self-governance exercised in a manner that is consistent with neoliberal domination;
- avoid complacency and remain responsive to changing calls for justice;
- demonstrate a willingness to take action in the name of justice, despite its complex and multifaceted character.

In mediation, restorative justice and reparations politics, there are some programmes that currently exhibit features of informal justice counterpublics.

While none fully meet this ideal, their existence is nonetheless testimony to the fact that a justice beyond the informal–formal justice complex may indeed be possible.

Civil mediation appears set upon a course of institutionalisation and professionalisation. Community mediation programmes, however, retain the potential to aspire toward becoming informal justice counterpublics. Within community mediation settings, individuals are, on occasion, empowered to reflect upon the broader community conditions that generate conflict. There is also no inherent limitation preventing these programmes from initiating self-corrective discussions on the ways in which juridical and neoliberal governmentalities might seep into their practices. If community mediation programmes are maintained as places of dialogic openness, and continue to seek out and eliminate manifest and latent forms of coercion, they will possess the communicative potential to foster understandings of justice and justice identities beyond those constituted by neoliberal and juridical norms. Along these lines, Coy and Hedeen (2005) point to the Cleveland Mediation Centre and the Community Dispute Resolution Centre of Ithaca, New York, as examples of organisations that have attempted to remain independent of the formal justice system (for example, by drawing on community-based referrals and multiple, including non-state, donors), that resist the imposition of a narrow judicial scope through their commitment to broader issues of social justice and that are alert to the 'co-optive pressures' of the informal–formal justice complex (Coy and Hedeen, 2005, p 427). Thus, a space is created that has the potential to allow for the production of counter-hegemonic notions of justice, so long as these community mediation programmes remain committed to protecting this space from juridical and neoliberal incursions. But such programmes would also need to find a means to move from being 'community mediation programmes' towards becoming 'mediation counterpublics' by identifying opportunities for political action to influence discussions within the wider public sphere and in policy-making institutions.

Under the rubric of restorative justice, efforts have been made to fashion programmes that better represent groups that are often excluded from formal justice practices. For example, the Youth Restorative Action Project (YRAP) in Edmonton, Alberta, is the result of the activism of young people seeking a place within justice discussions and decision making. The young people who designed and now administer the programme range in age from 14 to 21 years old, and represent a variety of life experiences and backgrounds (for example, honours students, recovering drug users and ex-offenders; Hogeveen, 2006, p 50). In the process of facilitating restorative sanctions in response to specific harms, YRAP also encourages criticisms of the cultural norms that silence the voice of youth in broader discussions of social justice, thus disrupting normative expectations that adults will be the key players in justice processes. YRAP has focused its efforts on those cases that dovetail with broader social issues, such as homelessness, racism and socio-economic inequality, thereby providing the programme with a framework for addressing structural injustices. Moreover, YRAP has remained guarded with regards to state involvement in, and support for, its activities. Initially, it sought referrals through distinctly informal networks that it established with formal justice gatekeepers. In so doing, it sought to achieve organisational independence prior to seeking state solicitation of these services. Finally, it has worked to maintain a degree of critical reflexivity so that its goals and values do not become compromised by its forays into the informal–formal justice complex (Hogeveen, 2006). It should be noted, however, that a judge must approve YRAP-designed sanctions and, although thus far judges have largely accepted its proposals, this adds an element of formal monitoring to YRAP procedures. It is also, at this point, unclear how YRAP programmes might fully become restorative justice counterpublics, disseminating to the broader public sphere the critical and counter-hegemonic understandings developed within its encounters.

Within reparations politics, victim and survivor-based movements have successfully mobilised to foment discussion of the denied or forgotten past, to destabilise imposed identities of 'terrorist' and 'defender', and to press for justice beyond hegemonic limits. Along these lines, many of the still-surviving 'comfort women', who hail from Korea, China and other nations subjugated by the Japanese in the 1930s and 1940s, have refused privately funded reparations and an unofficial apology from Japan. Their insistence is that a dialogue must be initiated within Japanese society about the injustices imposed upon them, bringing an end to the nationalist denial that has branded these women as willing 'prostitutes'. Likewise, the *Madres de Plaza de Mayo* (Mothers of the Plaza de Mayo) in Argentina have been relentless in their efforts to preserve the memory of their loved ones who were 'disappeared' by the Argentine military junta between 1976 and 1983. As a matter of principle, they have rejected individual reparations as 'blood money' and publicly denounced perpetrators of these crimes, despite a 1990 presidential pardon. In this sense, they have remained committed to their ideal of justice despite the social and political complexities that obstruct its realisation.

Reparations movements such as these are arenas for the expression and mobilisation of counter-memory, and serve to incite broader public discussion of their justice demands. In pursuit of this objective, it is not uncommon for proponents to resort to legal and political interventions to expand opportunities for justice, but it is in this effort that they risk dilution as they become embroiled within the informal–formal justice complex. As Sundquist notes in relation to African-American slavery reparations, legal actions, despite the threat of juridification, can serve to bring the concerns of the movement forward.

> Legal suits should not strive to achieve a modicum of success—however unlikely—by drafting narrow claims within the individual rights

paradigm. Rather, the legal claims must be broadly drafted to encompass all of the concerns critical to the transformative model. Although these legal suits may be vulnerable to dismissal for failing to state a legally cognizable claim, current and past legal cases that sought to fit within the individual rights paradigm have met with similar fates. Since the primary goal of the legal attack is to generate dialogue and awareness, critically drafted claims make the most sense.

(2003, p 694)

Sundquist thus suggests a tactical use of law designed to open space for an expansive discussion of justice, rather than simply to achieve individual recompense. Adopting this strategy would require that reparations movements resist the temptation to succumb to the ameliorative offerings of the state, unless some clear strategic benefit can be gained through such compromise.[2] Above all, however, in becoming reparations counterpublics, these movements must seek a path that allows them to 'keep going' towards their transformative goals, resisting immersion in a 'Thermidorian' politics (Badiou, 2005) that accepts a premature end point, loses its transformative energy and caves in under the very forces it set out to confront.[3]

Although promising, none of these examples of mediation, restorative justice and reparations politics fully meets the criteria of informal justice counterpublics. First, they are still largely passive and defensive publics, engrossed in the difficult task of protecting their discursive space, rather than that of making disruptive interventions within the informal–formal justice complex.[4] A second and related point is that their deliberative efforts appear premature, because they have not yet fully carved out the space required for open and unrestricted dialogue. Because they have not carried out sufficient oppositional activities to disrupt the informal–formal justice complex, their justice deliberations are often already formed by, and embedded within, the dominant

2   This is, admittedly, easier said than done. In some cases, the immediate needs of victims of mass violence and genocide are likely to outweigh political principles and an avenue must be found to meet these needs without fully compromising the group's justice ideals.

3   It should also be noted that informal justice counterpublics must also be responsive to the particular situation in which they operate. Reparations demands, for example, are often limited by the affirmative aspirations of the nation state. For this reason, the path toward transformative reparations does not necessarily begin in the same local settings that ground mediation and restorative justice. Instead, reparations may need to start out in the supranational domain of international politics, drawing on the auspices of institutions such as the United Nations, the International Criminal Court and even, perhaps, an international truth commission when these venues provide more potent opportunities for freeing reparative dialogues from restrictions.

4   This is less true for the examples of reparations politics presented above. The comfort women and the *Madres de Plaza de Mayo* have long participated in protest activities that are specifically designed to influence discussions within the broader public sphere and with the end goal of inspiring policy change.

logics of this complex. For these reasons, to become informal justice counterpublics, these programmes must find means of challenging both the dominant norms of the informal–formal justice complex (including the systemic
values that undergird them) and their own everyday practices. While most of
the examples listed above show evidence of self-reflexivity with regards to
their own practices, this reflexivity will be to no avail if the programmes do
not simultaneously expand the space of what is thinkable and practicable in
terms of justice in the broader social world.

These continuing challenges to the project of informal justice counterpublics bring us to a final example that illustrates the need for informal justice
counterpublics to engage strategically with the political realm in order to create an adequate space for the transformative justice that they envision. This
example, however, does not come from the world of already-institutionalised
informal justice practices, but rather from the 'postmodern revolutionary'
activities of the Zapatista National Liberation Army (EZLN, also 'Zapatistas'). On 1 January 1994, the EZLN stormed several towns in the southern
Mexican state of Chiapas. The indigenous Chiapanecos and Mexican rad-
icals who comprised their ranks declared that they did not seek state power or
revolution in any traditional sense; rather, their efforts were directed toward
awakening civil society and expanding the meaning of democracy within
Mexico. In particular, they sought to forge a space for the recognition of
indigenous rights and indigenous forms of economic and cultural life; they
saw this demand as interconnected with the grievances of multiple social
movements and invited others to join together in protest.

Most interesting, in respect of our concerns, is that they took a novel
approach to questions of crime and law. For example, upon capturing Division General Absalon Castellanos Dominguez, the EZLN issued a statement
charging the Division General with crimes that included repression, torture,
kidnapping, jailing, rape, murder, assassination of Chiapaneco people and
forcing the Chiapanecos to take arms in pursuit of justice. A tribunal of
masked Zapatistas issued the following sentence for these crimes:

> Division General Absalon Castellanos Dominguez is condemned to
> permanent imprisonment, and to doing manual work in an Indigenous
> community in Chiapas to earn his bread and the other things necessary
> for his subsistence. [However,] As a message to the people of Mexico
> and to the peoples and governments of the world, the Zapatista Justice
> Tribunal of the EZLN commutes the permanent imprisonment sentence
> of Division General Absalon Castellanos Dominguez, leaving him physi-
> cally free and, in place of his sentence, condemns him to live until his
> final days with the embarrassment and shame of having received the
> forgiveness and goodness of those who, for so much time, he humiliated,
> kidnapped, robbed, dispossessed and assassinated.
>
> (EZLN, quoted in Lippens, 2003, p 183)

A tension is evident here between the values of justice aspired to by the EZLN—a justice defined by 'forgiveness and goodness'—and its understanding of the necessity of militant action. In this manner, the goal of a communitarian and relational justice is brought forward through an adversarial struggle for rights. Aware that it faced a public sphere unresponsive to its grievances, the EZLN created a counterpublic in which matters of justice and indigenous rights could be discussed, and which could serve as a potent means for communicating these ideas to the mainstream public (for example, through the internet and other media). As Lippens (2003) notes, a space must be made for the negotiation and pursuit of justice, even if this means engaging in a seemingly self-contradictory position of embracing compromise while engaging in battle.

Building on these arguments, informal justice counterpublics require more than an unyielding dedication to a particular form of conflict resolution practice. We are not suggesting an armed informal justice insurrection, but protest actions, political alliances, acts of refusal in the face of state co-optation and similar radical (and adversarial) interventions needed to create space for meaningful informal deliberations and to influence discussions within the broader public sphere. In this manner, the goal is not simply to have 'mediation', or some other strategy of compromise, accepted within and by dominant social institutions, nor is it to protect sedimented values of informal justice from corruption. Rather, informal justice counterpublics must be designed to create sustainable opportunities for disruption, empowerment and social change—that is, a justice that allows participants mutually to address societal problems and social suffering in ways that are not prefigured or easily assimilated by the institutional guardians of juridical power.

Of course, such instantiations of transformative justice are rare, given the ubiquity of the informal–formal justice complex and the pervasive ideological grip of neoliberalism in contemporary capitalist society. But examples do occur, and only by wilfully following their inventive lead and remaining committed to the justice that they envision can we hope to achieve the kind of transformative change capable of shaking the informal–formal justice complex to its foundation.

References

Abel, RL, 'The contradictions of informal justice', in R Abel (ed) *The Politics of Informal Justice: The American Experience, Vol 1*, 1982, New York, NY: Academic Press, pp 267–320.

Acorn, AE, *Compulsory Compassion: A Critique of Restorative Justice*, 2004, Vancouver, BC: University of British Columbia Press.

Adam, H, 'Divided memories: confronting the crimes of previous regimes', *TELOS*, Winter 2000, 118, pp 87–109.

Ali, TM and Matthews, RO (eds), *Durable Peace: Challenges for Peacebuilding in Africa*, 2004, Toronto, ON: University of Toronto Press.

Allard, P and Northey, W, 'Christianity: the rediscovery of restorative justice', in G Johnstone (ed) *A Restorative Justice Reader: Texts, Sources, Context*, 2003, Cullompton: Willan Publishing, pp 158–70.

Alvarez, A, *Governments, Citizens and Genocide: A Comparative and Interdisciplinary Approach*, 2001, Indianapolis, IN: University of Indiana Press.

Amadiume, I and An-Na'im, A (eds), *The Politics of Memory: Truth, Healing and Social Justice*, 2000, London: Zed Books.

Amnesty International, *Gacaca: A Question of Justice*, 2002, accessed 22 February 2007, http://web.amnesty.org/library/pdf/AFR470072002ENGLISH/$File/AFR4700702.pdf.

Anderson, C, 'Governing aboriginal justice in Canada: constructing responsible individuals and communities through "tradition" ', *Crime, Law and Social Change*, 1999, 31:4, pp 303–26.

Andrews, EL, 'Germany accepts $5.1 billion accord to end claims of Nazi slave workers', *New York Times*, 18 December 1999, p A10.

Angus, I, *Emergent Publics: An Essay on Social Movements and Democracy*, 2001, Winnipeg, MB: Arbeiter Ring.

Antze, P and Lambek, M (eds), *Tense Past: Cultural Essays in Trauma and Memory*, 1996, New York, NY: Routledge.

Apel, KO, 'The problem of philosophical foundations grounding in light of a transcendental pragmatics of language', in K Baynes, J Bohman and T McCarthy (eds) *After Philosophy*, 1987, Cambridge MA: MIT Press, pp 250–90.

Arendt, H, *Eichmann in Jerusalem: A Report on the Banality of Evil*, 1963, New York, NY: The Viking Press.

Asch, M (ed), *Aboriginal and Treaty Rights in Canada: Essays on Laws, Equality, and Respect for Difference*, 1997, Vancouver, BC: University of British Columbia Press.

Auerbach, JS, *Justice Without Law? Resolving Disputes Without Lawyers*, 1983, New York, NY: Oxford University Press.

Augusti-Panareda, J, 'The possibility of personal empowerment in dispute resolution: Habermas, Foucault and community mediation', *Research in Social Movements, Conflicts and Change*, 2005, 26:IV, pp 265–90.

Austin-Broos, D, 'ATSIC undone: some local and national dimensions', *Australian Journal of Anthropology*, 2004, 15:3, pp 309–11.

Badiou, A, *Metapolitics*, 2005, London: Verso.

Barkan, E, *The Guilt of Nations: Restitution and Negotiating Historical Injustices*, 2000, New York, NY: WW Norton.

Barkan, E, 'Restitution and amending historical injustices in international morality', in J Torpey (ed) *Politics and the Past: On Repairing Historical Injustices*, 2003, Lanham, NJ: Rowman and Littlefield, pp 91–102.

Barnett, R, 'Restitution: a new paradigm of criminal justice', *Ethics*, 1977, 87:4, pp 279–301.

Barry, A, Osborne, T and Rose, N, 'Introduction', in A Barry, T Osborne and N Rose (eds) *Foucault and Political Reason: Liberalism, Neo-Liberalism and Rationalities of Government*, 1996, London: UCL Press, pp 1–17.

Bartholomew, A and Mayer, M, 'Nomads of the present: Melucci's contribution to "New Social Movement" theory', *Theory, Culture, and Society*, 1992, 9:4, pp 141–59.

Bauman, Z, *Community: Seeking Safety in an Insecure World*, 2001, Cambridge: Polity Press.

Bazemore, G and Umbreit, M, 'Rethinking the sanctioning function in juvenile court: retributive or restorative responses to youth crime', *Crime and Delinquency*, 1995, 41:3, pp 296–316.

Benhabib, S, *Situating the Self: Gender, Community and Postmodernism in Contemporary Ethics*, 1992, New York, NY: Routledge.

Benhabib, S, 'Toward a deliberative model of democratic legitimacy', in S Benhabib (ed) *Democracy and Difference: Contesting the Boundaries of the Political*, 1996, Princeton, NJ: Princeton University Press, pp 67–87.

Benjamin, W, *Illuminations*, H Arendt (ed) and H Zohn (trans) 1969, New York, NY: Shocken Books.

Bloxham, D, *Genocide on Trial: War Crimes Trials and the Formation of Holocaust History and Memory*, 2001, Oxford: Oxford University Press.

Bonta, J, Rooney, J and Wallace-Capretta, S, 'Restorative justice: an evaluation of the Restorative Resolutions Project', 1998, Ottawa, ON: Solicitor General of Canada.

Bourdieu, P, 'Structures, strategies, and the habitus', in C Lemert (ed) *French Sociology: Rapture and Renewal since 1968*, 1981, New York, NY: Columbia University Press, pp 86–96.

Bourdieu, P, 'The force of law: toward a sociology of the juridical field', *Hastings Law Journal*, 1987, 38:5, pp 805–53.

Bourdieu, P, *The Logic of Practice*, R Nice (trans), 1990, Cambridge: Polity Press.

Bourdieu, P, *Language and Symbolic Power*, G Raymond and M Adamson (trans), 1991, Cambridge, MA: Harvard University Press.

Braithwaite, J, *Crime, Shame and Reintegration*, 1989, Cambridge: Cambridge University Press.

Braithwaite, J, *Restorative Justice and a Better Future*, Dorothy J Killam Memorial Lecture, 17 October 1996, Halifax, NS: Dalhousie University.

Braithwaite, J, *Restorative Justice and Responsive Regulation*, 2002, New York, NY: Oxford University Press.

Braithwaite, J, 'Restorative justice and a better future' in G Johnstone (ed) *A Restorative Justice Reader: Texts, Sources, Context*, 2003, Cullompton: Willan Publishing, pp 83–198.

Braithwaite, J and Daly, K, 'Masculinities, violence and communitarian control', in T Newburn and E Stanko (eds) *Just Boys Doing Business? Men, Masculinities and Crime*, 1994, London: Routledge, pp 189–213.

Braithwaite, J and Mugford, S, 'Conditions of successful reintegration ceremonies: dealing with juvenile offenders', *British Journal of Criminology*, 1994, 34:2, pp 139–71.

Braithwaite, J and Petit, P, *Not Just Desserts: A Republican Theory of Criminal Justice*, 1990, Oxford: Clarendon Press.

Brigg, M, 'Mediation, power, and cultural difference', *Conflict Resolution Quarterly*, 2003, 20:3: pp 287–306.

Brooker, P, 'The "juridification" of alternative dispute resolution', *Anglo-American Law Review*, 1999, 28:1, pp 1–36.

Brooks, RL (ed), *When Sorry Isn't Enough: The Controversy Over Apologies and Reparations for Human Injustice*, 1999, New York, NY: New York University Press.

Brooks, RL, 'Reflections on reparations', in J Torpey (ed) *Politics and the Past: On Repairing Historical Injustices*, 2003, Lanham, NJ: Rowman and Littlefield, pp 103–16.

Browning, CR, *Ordinary Men: Reserve Police Battalion 101 and the Final Solution in Poland*, 1992, New York, NY: Harper Perennial.

Burchell, G, 'Liberal government and techniques of the self', *Economy and Society*, August 1993, 22:3, pp 267–82.

Burchell, G, Gordon, C and Miller, P (eds), *The Foucault Effect: Studies in Governmentality with Two Lectures by and an Interview with Michel Foucault*, 1991, Chicago, IL: University of Chicago Press.

Burger, Chief Justice Warren, 'Address Before the National Conference on the Causes of Popular Dissatisfaction with the Administration of Justice, April 7–9, 1976', reprinted in AL Levin and RR Wheeler (eds) *The Pound Conference: Perspectives on Justice in the Future*, 1979, St Paul, Minneapolis, MN: West Publishing Co.

Bush, RAB and Folger, JP, *The Promise of Mediation: The Transformative Approach to Conflict*, rev'd edn, 1994, San Francisco, CA: Jossey-Bass.

Byrne, S, Senehi, J, Sandole, D and Staroste-Sandole, I (eds), *Conflict Resolution: Core Concepts, Theories, Approaches and Practices*, 2007, London: Routledge.

Cain, M and Harrington, CB (eds), *Lawyers in a Postmodern World: Translation and Transgression*, 1994, Buckingham: Open University Press.

Cairns, A, 'Coming to terms with the past', in J Torpey (ed) *Politics and the Past: On Repairing Historical Injustices*, 2003, Lanham, NJ: Rowman and Littlefield, pp 63–90.

Calder v Attorney-General Of British Columbia (1973) 34 DLR (3d) 145; [1973] SCR 313; [1973] 4 WWR 1.

Calhoun, C (ed), *Habermas and the Public Sphere*, 1992, Cambridge, MA: MIT Press.

Cauvin, HE, 'World briefing—Africa: Namibia: a century later, tribe sues', *New York Times*, 7 September 2001, http://query.nytimes.com/gst/ fullpage.html?res= 9E02E2DF1139F934A3575AC0A9679C8B63&n=Top%2fRefrence%2fTimes%20 Topics%2fSubjects% 2fR%2fReparations.

Cayley, D, *The Expanding Prison: The Crisis in Crime and Punishment*, 1998, Toronto, ON: House of Anansi Press.

Charbonneau, S, 'The Canadian Youth Criminal Justice Act 2003: a step forward for advocates of restorative justice?', in E Elliott and RM Gordon (eds) *New Directions in Restorative Justice: Issues, Practice, Evaluation*, 2004, Cullompton: Willan Publishing, pp 75–88.

Chilton, S and Cuzzo, MSW, 'Habermas's theory of communicative action as a theoretical framework for mediation practice', *Conflict Resolution Quarterly*, 2005, 22:3, pp 325–48.

Christie, N, 'Conflicts as property', *British Journal of Criminology*, 1977, 17:1, pp 1–15.

Christodoulidis, EA, ' "Truth and reconciliation" as risks', *Social and Legal Studies*, 2000, 9:2, pp 179–204.

Cobb, S and Rifkin, J, 'Practice and paradox: deconstructing neutrality in mediation', *Law and Social Inquiry*, 1991, 16:1, pp 35–62.

Cohen, S, *Visions of Social Control: Crime, Punishment, and Classification*, 1985, Cambridge: Polity Press.

Cohen, S, *States of Denial: Knowing About Atrocities and Suffering*, 2001, Cambridge: Polity Press.

Cole, T, *Selling the Holocaust: From Auschwitz to Schindler How History is Bought, Packaged, and Sold*, 1999, New York, NY: Routledge.

Consedine, J, *Restorative Justice: Healing the Effects of Crime*, 1995, Lyttleton, NZ: Ploughshares.

Consedine, J, 'The Maori restorative tradition', in G Johnstone (ed) *A Restorative Justice Reader: Texts, Sources, Context*, 2003, Cullompton: Willan Publishing, pp 152–7.

Cornell, D, Rosenfeld, M and Carlson, DG (eds), *Deconstruction and the Possibility of Justice*, 1992, London: Routledge.

Coy, PG and Hedeen, T, 'A stage model of social movement co-optation: community mediation in the United States', *The Sociological Quarterly*, Summer 2005, 46:3, pp 405–35.

Cragg, W, *The Practice of Punishment: Towards a Theory of Restorative Justice*, 1992, London: Routledge.

Crawford, A, 'In the hands of the public?', in G Johnstone (ed) *A Restorative Justice Reader: Texts, Sources, Context*, 2003, Cullompton: Willan Publishing, pp 312–19.

Crawford, A and Newburn, T, 'Recent developments in restorative justice for young people in England and Wales: community participation and representation', *British Journal of Criminology*, 2002, 42:3, pp 476–85.

Crossley, N, 'On systematically distorted communication: Bourdieu and the socio-analysis of publics', in N Crossley and JM Roberts (eds) *After Habermas: New Perspectives on the Public Sphere*, 2004, Newcastle: Blackwell Publishing, pp 88–112.

Dallaire, R and Beardsley, B, *Shake Hands with the Devil: The Failure of Humanity in Rwanda*, 2003, Toronto, ON: Random House Canada.

Daly, K and Immarigeon, R, 'The past, present, and future of restorative justice: some critical reflections', *Contemporary Justice Review*, 1998, 1:1, pp 21–45.

Delgamuukw v British Columbia 1997, 3 SCR 1010 (SCC).

Derrida, J, 'Force of law: the "mystical foundation of authority" ', in D Cornell, M Rosenfeld and DG Carlson (eds) *Deconstruction and the Possibility of Justice*, 1992, London: Routledge, pp 3–67.

Des Forges, A, *Leave None to Tell the Story: Genocide in Rwanda*, 1999, New York, NY: Human Rights Watch.

Dezalay, Y, 'The forum should fit the fuss: the economics and politics of negotiated justice', in M Cain and CB Harrington (eds) *Lawyers in a Postmodern World: Translation and Transgression*, 1994, Buckingham: Open University Press, pp 155–82.

Diani, M, 'The concept of social movement', *The Sociological Review*, 1992, 40:1, pp 1–25.

Diefendorf, JM (ed), *Lessons and Legacies IV: New Currents in Holocaust Research*, 2004, Evanston, IL: Northwestern University Press.

Doubt, K, *Sociology After Bosnia and Kosovo: Recovering Justice*, 2000, Lanham, MD: Rowman and Littlefield.

Dryzek, JS, *Deliberative Democracy and Beyond*, 2000, Oxford: Oxford University Press.

Duguid, S, *Can Prisons Work? The Prisoner as Object and Subject in Modern Corrections*, 2000, Toronto, ON: University of Toronto Press.

Dzur, AW and Olson, SM, 'The value of community participation in restorative justice', *Journal of Social Philosophy*, Spring 2004, XXXV:1, pp 91–107.

Elliott, E and Gordon, RM (eds) *New Directions in Restorative Justice: Issues, Practice, Evaluation*, 2004, Cullompton: Willan Publishing.

Ewick, P and Silbey, SS, *The Common Place of Law: Stories of Popular Legal Consciousness*, 1998, Chicago, IL: University of Chicago Press.

Falk, RA, *Human Rights Horizons: The Pursuit of Justice in a Globalizing World*, 2000, New York, NY: Routledge.

Fisher, R and Ury, W, *Getting to Yes: Negotiating Agreement Without Giving In*, 2nd edn, 1991, New York, NY: Penguin Books.

Fishkin, JS, *Democracy and Deliberation: New Directions for Democratic Reform*, 1991, New Haven, CT: Yale University Press.

Fitzpatrick, P, 'The rise and rise of informalism', in R Matthews (ed) *Informal Justice?*, 1988, London: Sage, pp 178–98.

Fitzpatrick, P, 'The impossibility of popular justice', in SE Merry and N Milner (eds) *The Possibility of Popular Justice: A Case Study of Community Mediation in the United States*, 1995, Ann Arbor, MI: University of Michigan Press, pp 453–74.

Folger, J and Bush, RAB, 'A response to Gaynier's "Transformative Mediation": in search of a theory of practice', *Conflict Resolution Quarterly*, 2005, 23:1, pp 123–7.

Foucault, M, *Discipline and Punish: The Birth of the Prison*, 1977, New York, NY: Pantheon Books.

Foucault, M, *The History of Sexuality, Vol 1: An Introduction*, 1985, New York, NY: Vintage Books.

Foucault, M, *The History of Sexuality, Vol 3: The Care of the Self*, 1988, New York, NY: Vintage Books.

Foucault, M, *The History of Sexuality, Vol 2: The Use of Pleasure*, 1990, New York, NY: Vintage Books.

Foucault, M, 'Governmentality', in G Burchell, C Gordon and P Miller (eds) *The Foucault Effect: Studies in Governmentality with Two Lectures by and an Interview with Michel Foucault*, 1991, Chicago, IL: University of Chicago Press, pp 87–104.

Foucault, M, *Ethics, Subjectivity and Truth*, Paul Rabinow (ed), 1994, New York, NY: The New Press.

Fraser, N, 'Rethinking the public sphere: a contribution to the critique of actually existing democracy', in C Calhoun (ed) *Habermas and the Public Sphere*, 1992, Cambridge, MA: MIT Press, pp 109–42.

Fraser, N, *Justice Interruptus: Critical Reflections on the 'Postsocialist Condition'*, 1997, New York, NY: Routledge.

Fuller, L, 'Mediation—its forms and functions', *South California Law Review*, 1971, 44, pp 305–39.

Garfinkel, H, 'Conditions of successful degradation ceremonies', *American Journal of Sociology*, 1956, 61:5, pp 420–4.

Garland, D, *The Culture of Control: Crime and Social Order in Contemporary Society*, 2001, Chicago, IL: University of Chicago Press.

Garland, D and Sparks, R, 'Criminology, social theory and the challenge of our times', *British Journal of Criminology*, 2000, 40:2, pp 189–204.

Gilson, RJ and Mnookin, RH, 'Disputing through agents: cooperation and conflict between lawyers in litigation', *Columbia Law Review*, 1994, 94, pp 509–66.

Glaister, A, 'Mediation trends in the north of England', 2001, accessed 10 January 2007, http://www.mediate.com/articles/glaister.cfm#.

Goldhagen, DJ, *Hitler's Willing Executioners: Ordinary Germans and the Holocaust*, 1996, New York, NY: Vintage Books.

Goldhagen, DJ, *A Moral Reckoning: The Role of the Catholic Church in the Holocaust and its Unfulfilled Duty of Repair*, 2003, New York, NY: Knopf.

Goldschmidt, S, *Legal Claims Against Germany*, 1945, New York, NY: The Dryden Press.

Goschler, C, 'German compensation to Jewish Nazi victims', in JM Diefendorf (ed) *Lessons and Legacies IV: New Currents in Holocaust Research*, 2004, Evanston, IL: Northwestern University Press, pp 219–49.

Gutmann, A (ed), *Multiculturalism and the Politics of Recognition*, 1992, Princeton, NJ: Princeton University Press.

Habermas, J, *The Theory of Communicative Action: Reason and the Rationalization of Society, Vol I*, 1984, Boston, MA: Beacon Press.

Habermas, J, *The Structural Transformation of the Public Sphere*, 1989, Cambridge: Polity Press.

Habermas, J, *Moral Consciousness and Communicative Action*, C Lenhardt and SW Nicholsen (trans), 1990, Cambridge, MA: MIT Press.

Habermas, J, 'Struggles for recognition in the democratic constitutional state', in A Gutmann (ed) *Multiculturalism*, 1994, Princeton, NJ: Princeton University Press, pp 107–48.

Habermas, J, *Between Facts and Norms: Contributions to a Discourse Theory of Law and Democracy*, W Rehg (trans), 1999, Cambridge, MA: MIT Press.

Hacking, I, 'Memory sciences, memory politics', in P Antze and M Lambek (eds) *Tense Past: Cultural Essays in Trauma and Memory*, 1996, New York, NY: Routledge.

Harnett, B, *Put the Law on Your Side: Strategies for Winning the Legal Game*, 1985, San Diego, CA: Harcourt Brace Jovanovich.

Harrington, CB, *Shadow Justice: The Ideology and Institutionalization of Alternatives to Court*, 1985, Westport, CT: Greenwood Press.

Harrington, CB and Merry, SE, 'The ideology of community mediation', *Law and Society Review*, 1988, 22:4, pp 709–35.

Hayner, PB, *Unspeakable Truths: Facing the Challenge of Truth Commissions*, 2002, New York and London: Routledge.

Hedeen, T and Coy, PG, 'Community mediation and the court system: the ties that bind', *Mediation Quarterly*, 2000, 17:4, pp 351–67.

Hein, L, 'War compensation: claims against the Japanese government and Japanese corporations for war crimes', in J Torpey (ed) *Politics and the Past: On Repairing Historical Injustices*, 2003, Lanham, MD: Rowman and Littlefield, pp 127–48.

Herf, J, *Divided Memory: The Nazi Past in the Two Germanys*, 1997, Cambridge, MA: Harvard University Press.

Heydebrand, W, 'Process rationality as legal governance: a comparative perspective', *International Sociology*, June 2003, 18:2, pp 325–49.

Hinkson, J, 'Subjectivity and neo-liberal economy', *Arena Journal*, 1998, 11, pp 119–44.

Hofrichter, R, 'Neighborhood justice and the social control problems of American capitalism: a perspective', in R Abel (ed) *The Politics of Informal Justice: The American Experience, Vol 1*, 1982, New York, NY: Academic Press, pp 207–48.

Hofrichter, R, *Neighborhood Justice in Capitalist Society: The Expansion of the Informal State*, 1987, New York, NY: Greenwood.

Hogeveen, B, 'Unsettling youth justice and cultural norms: the Youth Restorative Action Project', *Journal of Youth Studies*, 2006, 9:1, pp 47–66.

Homeowner Protection Office, 'Province announces notice to mediate process for residential construction disputes', 31 May 1999, http://www.hpo.bc.ca/News Releases/05–27–99.htm.

Horkheimer, M and Adorno, T, *Dialectic of Enlightenment*, 1976, New York, NY: Continuum International Publishing Group.

Hudson, B, 'Restorative justice: the challenge of sexual and racial violence', in G Johnstone (ed) *A Restorative Justice Reader: Texts, Sources, Context*, 2003, Cullompton: Willan Publishing, pp 438–50.

Human Rights Watch, 'US: Ashcroft attacks human rights law—justice department undermining key precedent', *Human Rights News*, 15 May 2003, accessed 25 May 2003, www.hrw.org/press/2003/05/us051503.htm.

Illich, I, *Towards a History of Needs*, 1977, New York, NY: Pantheon Books.

Illich, I, Zola, I, McKnight, J and Shaiken, H, *Disabling Professions*, 1977, London: Marion Boyars.

International Military Tribunal, *Trial of the Major War Criminals Before the International Military Tribunal, Nuremberg, 14 November 1945–1 October 1946*, 1995, Buffalo, NY: William S Hein.

Jay, M, *The Dialectical Imagination: A History of the Frankfurt School and The Institute of Social Research, 1923–1950*, 1973, Berkeley, CA: University of California Press.

John Doe I, et al v Unocal Corporation et al (2003) 'Brief for the United States of America as Amicus Curiae', in the United States Court of Appeals for the Ninth Circuit, Nos 00–56603, 00–56628.

Johnstone, G, *Restorative Justice: Ideas, Values, Debates*, 2002, Cullompton: Willan Publishing.

Johnstone, G, 'Introduction: restorative approaches to criminal justice', in G Johnstone (ed) *A Restorative Justice Reader: Texts, Sources, Context*, 2003, Cullompton: Willan Publishing, pp 1–18.

Jones, A, *Genocide: A Comprehensive Introduction*, 2006, London and New York: Routledge.

Jones, DL, 'Mediation, conflict resolution and critical theory', *Review of International Studies*, 2000, 26:4, pp 647–62.

Keane, J (ed), *Civil Society and the State: New European Perspectives*, 1994, London: Verso.

Kim, H, 'German reparations: institutionalized insufficiency', in RL Brooks (ed) *When Sorry Isn't Enough: The Controversy over Apologies and Reparations for Human Injustice*, 1999, New York, NY: New York University Press, pp 77–80.

Kriesberg, L and Misztal, B (eds), *Research in Social Movements, Conflicts and Change, Vol 10*, 1988, Greenwich: JAI Press.

Kritz, NJ, *Transitional Justice: How Emerging Democracies Reckon with Former Regimes*, 1995, Washington DC, WA: United States Institute of Peace Press.

Kueneman, R, 'The origins and role of law in society', in R Linden (ed) *Criminology: A Canadian Perspective, Vol 5*, 2004, Toronto, ON: Thomson-Nelson, pp 20–54.

Langer, R, 'The juridification and technicisation of alternative dispute resolution practices', *Canadian Journal of Law and Society*, Spring 1998, 13:1, pp 169–87.

Laroque, E, 'Re-examining culturally appropriate models in criminal justice applications', in M Asch (ed) *Aboriginal and Treaty Rights in Canada: Essays on Laws, Equality, and Respect for Difference*, 1997, Vancouver, BC: University of British Columbia Press, pp 75–96.

Lee, O, 'Culture and democratic theory: toward a theory of symbolic democracy', *Constellations*, 1998, 5:4, pp 433–55.

Lemert, C (ed) *French Sociology: Rapture and Renewal since 1968*, 1981, New York, NY: Columbia University Press.

Levin, AL and Wheeler, RR (eds) *The Pound Conference: Perspectives on Justice in the Future*, 1979, St Paul, Minneapolis, MN: West Publishing Co.

Levrant, S, Cullen, FT, Fulton, B and Wozniak, JF, 'Reconsidering restorative justice: the corruption of benevolence revisited?', *Crime and Delinquency*, 1999, 45:1, pp 3–27.

Lewis, NA, 'Agreement sets up rules for Holocaust claims', *New York Times*, 20 September 2002, http://query.nytimes.com/gst/fullpage.html?res=9C06E2DF1130 F933A1575AC0A9649C8B63.

Linden, R (ed), *Criminology: A Canadian Perspective, Vol 5*, 2004, Toronto, ON: Thomson-Nelson.

Lippens, R, 'The imaginary of Zapatista punishment and justice: speculations from the "first postmodern revolution" ', *Punishment and Society*, 2003, 5:2, pp 179–95.

Long, WJ and Brecke, P, *War and Reconciliation: Reason and Emotion in Conflict Resolution*, 2002, Cambridge, MA: MIT Press.

Longman, T, 'Obstacles to peacebuilding in Rwanda', in TM Ali and RO Matthews (eds) *Durable Peace: Challenges for Peacebuilding in Africa*, 2004, Toronto, ON: University of Toronto Press, pp 61–85.

Maier, CS, *The Unmasterable Past: History, Holocaust, and German National Identity*, 1988, Cambridge, MA: Harvard University Press.

Maier, CS, 'Overcoming the past? Narrative and negotiation, remembering and reparation: issues at the interface of law and history', in J Torpey (ed) *Politics and the Past: On Repairing Historical Injustices*, 2003, Lanham, MD: Rowman and Littlefield, pp 295–304.

Mamdani, M, 'The truth according to the TRC', in I Amadiume and A An-Na'im (eds) *The Politics of Memory: Truth, Healing and Social Justice*, 2000, London: Zed Books, pp 176–83.

Mamdani, M, *When Victims Become Killers: Colonialism, Nativism, and the Genocide in Rwanda*, 2001, Princeton, NJ: Princeton University Press.

Mann, M, *The Dark Side of Democracy: Explaining Ethnic Cleansing*, 2005, Cambridge: Cambridge University Press.

Mansbridge, J, 'Using power/fighting power: the polity', in S Benhabib (ed) *Democracy and Difference: Contesting the Boundaries of the Political*, 1996, Princeton, NJ: Princeton University Press, pp 46–66.

Margalit, G, *Germany and its Gypsies: A Post-Auschwitz Ordeal*, 2002, Madison, WI: University of Wisconsin Press.

Marshall, TF, 'Restorative justice on trial in Britain', *Mediation Quarterly*, Spring 1995, 12:3, pp 217–31.

Marshall, TF, 'Restorative justice: an overview', in G Johnstone (ed) *A Restorative Justice Reader: Texts, Sources, Context*, 2003, Cullompton: Willan Publishing, pp 28–45.

Martinson, R, 'What works?—Questions and answers about prison reform', *The Public Interest*, Spring 1974, pp 22–54.

Mason, MA, *The Custody Wars: Why Children are Losing the Legal Battle and What We Can do About It*, 1999, New York, NY: Basic Books.

Matthews, R (ed), *Informal Justice?*, 1988, London: Sage.

McCarthy, JD and Zald, MN, *The Trend of Social Movements in America: Professionalization and Resource Mobilization*, 1973, Morristown, NJ: General Learning Corp.

McCarthy, JD and Zald, MN, 'Resource mobilization and social movements: a partial theory', *American Journal of Sociology*, 1977, 82:6, pp 1212–39.

McCarthy, T, 'Coming to terms with our past, part II: on the morality and politics of reparations for slavery', *Political Theory*, 2004, 32:6, pp 750–72.

McCold, P and Wachtel, B, 'Community is not a place: a new look at community justice initiatives', *Contemporary Justice Review*, 1998, 1:1, pp 71–85.

Melucci, A, *Nomads of the Present: Social Movements and Individual Needs in Contemporary Society*, 1987, Philadelphia, PA: Temple University Press.

Melucci, A, 'Social movements and the democratization of everyday life', in J Keane (ed) *Civil Society and the State: New European Perspectives*, 1994, London: Verso, pp 245–60.

Melucci, A, *Challenging Codes: Collective Action in the Information Age*, 1995, Cambridge: Cambridge University Press.

Menkel-Meadow, C, 'The many ways of mediation: the transformation of tradition, ideologies, paradigms, and practices—review essay', *Negotiation Journal*, 1995, 11:3, pp 217–42.

Merry, SE and Milner, N (eds), *The Possibility of Popular Justice: A Case Study of Community Mediation in the United States*, 1995, Ann Arbor, MI: University of Michigan Press.

Meyer, KE, 'Just how sorry can you get? Pretty sorry', *New York Times*, 29 November 1997, p B7.

Michalowski, R, *Law, Order and Crime*, 1985, New York, NY: Random House.

Military Government of Germany, United States Area of Control, Law No 59, in *Property Control: History, Policies, Practices and Procedures of the United States Area of Control, Germany*, 1948, unpublished German government document.

Miller, P and Rose, N, 'Governing economic life', *Economy and Society*, February 1990, 19:1, pp 1–31.

Miller, P and Rose, N, 'Political power beyond the state: problematics of the government', *British Journal of Sociology*, 1992, 43:2, pp 173–205.

Minow, M, *Between Vengeance and Forgiveness: Facing Genocide and Mass Violence*, 1998, Boston, MA: Beacon Press.

Misztal, BA, 'The sacralization of memory', *European Journal of Social Theory*, 2004, 7:1, pp 67–84.

Mnookin, RH and Kornhauser, L, 'Bargaining in the shadow of the law: the case of divorce', *Yale Law Journal*, 1979, 88:5, pp 950–97.

Moore, DB and O'Connell, TA, 'Family conferencing in Wagga Wagga: a communitarian model of justice', in G Johnstone (ed) *A Restorative Justice Reader: Texts, Sources, Contexts*, 2003, Cullompton: Willan Publishing, pp 212–24.

Morris, AD and McClurg Mueller, C (eds), *Frontiers in Social Movement Theory*, 1992, New Haven, CT: Yale University Press.

Morris, C and Pirie, A (eds), *Qualifications for Dispute Resolution: Perspectives on the Debate*, 1994, Victoria, BC: University of Victoria Institute for Dispute Resolution.

Morrison, B, 'Restorative justice in schools', in E Elliott and RM Gordon (eds) *New Directions in Restorative Justice: Issues, Practice, Evaluation*, 2005, Cullompton: Willan Publishing, pp 26–52.

Moses, S, *Jewish Post-War Claims*, 1944, Tel Aviv: Irgun Olej Merkaz Europa.

Nagy, R, 'Reconciliation in post-Commission South Africa: thick and thin accounts of solidarity', *Canadian Journal of Political Science*, June 2002, 35:2, pp 323–46.

Nesic, M, 'Mediation: on the rise in the United Kingdom', *Bond Law Review*, 2001, 13, p 2.

Newburn, T and Stanko, E (eds), *Just Boys Doing Business? Men, Masculinities and Crime*, 1994, London: Routledge.

Noble, C, 'Options in conflict management system design', *Workplace News*, May 2002, 8:5, p 5.

Novick, P, *The Holocaust in American Life*, 1999, Boston, MA: Mariner Books.

Offe, C, *Varieties of Transition: The East European and East German Experience*, 1997, Cambridge, MA: MIT Press.

Olson, SM and Dzur, AW, 'Revisiting informal justice: restorative justice and democratic professionalism', *Law and Society Review*, 2004, 38:1, pp 139–76.

Pakulski, J, 'Social movements in comparative perspective', in L Kriesberg and B Misztal (eds) *Research in Social Movements, Conflicts and Change, Vol 10*, 1988, Greenwich: JAI Press, pp 247–67.

Parkinson, J and Roche, D, 'Restorative justice: deliberative democracy in action?', *Australian Journal of Political Science*, 2004, 39:3, pp 505–18.

Pavlich, G, *Justice Fragmented: Mediating Community Disputes Under Postmodern Conditions*, 1996a, London: Routledge.

Pavlich, G, 'The power of community mediation: government and formation of self', *Law and Society Review*, 1996b, 30:4, pp 101–27.

Pavlich, G, 'Preventing crime: "social" versus "community" governance in Aotearoa/ New Zealand', in R Smandych (ed) *Governable Places: Readings on Governmentality and Crime Control*, 1999, Aldershot: Ashgate, pp 75–102.

Pavlich, G, 'The force of community', in H Strang and J Braithwaite (eds) *Restorative Justice and Civil Society*, 2001, Cambridge: Cambridge University Press, pp 56–68.

Pavlich, G, *Governing Paradoxes of Restorative Justice*, 2005, London: GlassHouse Press.

Peachey, DE, 'The Kitchener experiment', in G Johnstone (ed) *A Restorative Justice Reader: Texts, Sources, Context*, 2003, Cullompton: Willan Publishing, pp 178–86.

Pensky, M, 'On the use and abuse of memory: Habermas, "anamnestic solidarity", and the *Historikerstreit*', *Philosophy and Social Criticism*, 1989, 15:4, pp 351–81.

Picard, CA, *Mediating Interpersonal and Small Group Conflict*, 1998, Ottawa, ON: Golden Dog Press.

Plapinger, E and Stienstra, D, *ADR and Settlement in the Federal District Courts: A Sourcebook for Judges and Lawyers*, 1996, Washington DC, WA: Federal Judicial Center and CPR Institute for Dispute Resolution.

Pollard, Sir Charles, ' "If your only tool is a hammer, all your problems will look like nails" ', in H Strang and J Braithwaite (eds) *Restorative Justice and Civil Society*, 2000, Cambridge: Cambridge University Press, pp 165–79.

Power, S, *A Problem from Hell: America and the Age of Genocide*, 2002, New York, NY: Basic Books.

Pratt, J, 'The return of the wheelbarrow men—or, the arrival of postmodern penalty?', *British Journal of Criminology*, 2002, 40:1, pp 127–45.

Presser, L, 'Justice here and now: a personal reflection on the restorative and community justice paradigms', *Contemporary Justice Review*, March 2004, 7:1, pp 101–6.

Pross, C, *Paying for the Past: The Struggle over Reparations for Surviving Victims of the Nazi Terror*, 1998, Baltimore, MD: Johns Hopkins University Press.

Putnam, R, *Bowling Alone: The Collapse and Revival of American Community*, 2000, New York, NY: Touchstone.

Puxon, G, 'Gypsies seek reparations', *Patterns of Prejudice*, 1981, 15, pp 21–5.

Ratner, RS, 'Communicative rationality in the Citizens' Assembly and referendum processes', in ME Warren and H Pearse (eds) *Designing Democratic Renewal: The British Columbia Citizens' Assembly*, 2007, Cambridge: University of Cambridge Press, pp 254–86.

Ratner, RS, Carroll, WK and Woolford, A, 'Wealth of nations: aboriginal treaty-making in the era of globalization', in J Torpey (ed) *Politics and the Past: On Repairing Historical Injustices*, 2003, Lanham, MD: Rowman and Littlefield, pp 217–47.

Ratner, RS and Woolford, A, 'The persistent verticality problem in restorative justice', presented at the 73rd Annual Meeting of the Pacific Sociological Association, Hyatt Regency Hotel, Vancouver, BC, April 2002.

Rifkin, J, Millen, J and Cobb, S, 'Toward a new discourse for mediation: a critique of neutrality', *Mediation Quarterly*, Winter 1991, 9:2, pp 151–64.

Rigby, A, *Justice and Reconciliation: After the Violence*, 2001, Boulder, CO: Lynne Rienner.

Robinson, N, *Indemnification and Reparations—Jewish Aspects*, 1944, New York, NY: Institute of Jewish Affairs.

Rose, N, 'Government, authority and expertise in advanced liberalism', *Economy and Society*, August 1993, 22:3, pp 283–99.

Rose, N, 'Governing "advanced" liberal democracies', in A Barry, T Osborne and N Rose (eds) *Foucault and Political Reason: Liberalism, Neo-Liberalism and Rationalities of Government*, 1996, London: UCL Press, pp 37–64.

Rose, N, *Powers of Freedom: Reframing Political Thought*, 1999, Cambridge: Cambridge University Press.

Ross, R, *Returning to the Teachings: Exploring Aboriginal Justice*, 1996, Toronto, ON: Penguin Group of Canada.

Royal Commission on Aboriginal Peoples, *Report of the Royal Commission on Aboriginal Peoples*, 5 vols, 1996, Ottawa, ON: Canada Communications Group.

Ruggiero, V, South, N and Taylor, I (eds), *The New European Criminology: Crime and Social Order in Europe*, 1999, London: Routledge.

Sagi, N, *German Reparations: A History of the Negotiations*, 1980, Jerusalem: Hebrew University Magnes Press.

Schrafstetter, S, 'The diplomacy of *Wiedergutmachung*: memory, the Cold War, and the Western European victims of Nazism, 1956–1964', *Holocaust and Genocide Studies*, Winter 2003, 17:3, pp 459–79.

Scott, A, *Ideology and the New Social Movements*, 1990, London: Unwin Human.

Seamone, ER, 'Bringing a smile to mediation's two faces: how aspiring mediators might jump-start careers immediately following law school', Economics of Law Practice Seminar, University of Iowa College of Law Iowa City, 2 November 2000, accessed 23 January 2003, http://www.uiowa.edu/~cyberlaw/elp00/.

Selva, LH and Böhm, RM, 'A critical examination of the informalism experiment in the administration of justice', *Crime and Social Justice*, 1987, 29, pp 43–57.

Shabani, OAP, *Democracy, Power, and Legitimacy: The Critical Theory of Jurgen Habermas*, 2003, Toronto, ON: University of Toronto Press.

Shapland, J, Atkinson, A, Atkinson, H, Colledge, E, Dignan, J, Howes, M, Johnstone, J, Robinson, G and Sorsby, A, 'Situating restorative justice within criminal justice', *Theoretical Criminology*, 2006, 10:4, pp 505–32.

Shearing, C, 'Punishment and the changing face of governance', *Punishment and Society*, 2001, 3:2, pp 203–20.

Shearing, C and Kempa, M, 'A museum of hope: a story of Robben Island', *Annals AAPSS*, March 2004, 592, pp 62–78.

Sherman, L, 'Two Protestant ethics and the spirit of restoration', in H Strang and J Braithwaite (eds) *Restorative Justice and Civil Society*, 2001, Cambridge: Cambridge University Press, pp 35–55.

Shonholtz, R, 'Neighborhood justice systems: work, structure and guiding principles', *Mediation Quarterly*, 1984, 5, pp 3–30.

Smandych, R (ed), *Governable Places: Readings on Governmentality and Crime Control*, 1999, Aldershot: Ashgate.

Smith, RW, 'Human destructiveness and politics: the twentieth century as an age of genocide', in I Wallimann and MN Dobkowski (eds) *Genocide and the Modern Age: Etiology and Case Studies of Mass Death*, 1987, Syracuse, NY: Syracuse University Press, pp 21–40.

Snow, D and Benford, RD, 'Master frames and cycles of protest', in AD Morris and C McClurg Mueller (eds) *Frontiers in Social Movement Theory*, 1992, New Haven, CT: Yale University Press, pp 133–55.

Snow, DA, Rochford Jr, EB, Worden, SK and Benford, RD, 'Frame alignment process, micromobilization and movement participation', *American Sociological Review*, 1986, 51:4, pp 464–81.

Stanley, E, 'Truth commissions and the recognition of state crime', *British Journal of Criminology*, 2005, 45:4, pp 582–97.

Strang, H and Braithwaite, J, *Restorative Justice and Civil Society*, 2001, Cambridge: Cambridge University Press.

Sullivan, D, Tifft, L and Cordella, P, 'The phenomenon of restorative justice', *Contemporary Justice Review*, 1998, 1:1, pp 1–14.

Sundquist, C, 'Critical praxis, spirit healing, and community activism: preserving a subversive dialogue on reparations', *NYU Annual Survey of American Law*, 2003, 58:4, pp 659–98.

Tavuchis, N, *Mea Culpa: A Sociology of Apology and Reconciliation*, 1991, Stanford, CA: Stanford University Press.

Taylor, C, 'The politics of recognition', in A Gutmann (ed) *Multiculturalism and the Politics of Recognition*, 1992, Princeton, NJ: Princeton University Press, pp 25–74.

Teitel, R, *Transitional Justice*, 2000, New York, NY: Oxford University Press.

Tennant, P, *Aboriginal Peoples and Politics*, 1990, Vancouver, BC: University of British Columbia Press.

Thompson, J, *Taking Responsibility for the Past: Reparation and Historical Justice*, 2002, Cambridge: Polity Press.

Tickell, A and Peck, JA, 'Social regulation after Fordism: regulation theory, neoliberalism and the global–local nexus', *Economy and Society*, August 1995, 24:3, pp 357–86.

Tomasic, R, 'Mediation as an alternative to adjudication: rhetoric and reality in the Neighborhood Justice Movement', in R Tomasic and MM Feeley (eds) *Neighborhood Justice: Assessment of an Emerging Idea*, 1982, New York, NY: Longman.

Torpey, J, ' "Making whole what has been smashed": reflections on reparations', *Journal of Modern History*, June 2001, 73:2, pp 333–58.

Torpey, J, 'Introduction', in J Torpey (ed) *Politics and the Past: On Repairing Historical Injustices*, 2003, Lanham, NJ: Rowman and Littlefield.

Torpey, J, *Making Whole What has Been Smashed: On Reparations Politics*, 2006, Cambridge, MA: Harvard University Press.

Tutu, D, *No Future Without Forgiveness*, 2000, New York, NY: Image, Doubleday.

Umbreit, M and Zehr, H, 'Restorative family group conferences: differing models and guidelines for practice', *Federal Probation*, 1996, 60:3, pp 24–9.

United Nations, *Handbook of Restorative Justice Programs*, 2007, New York, NY: United Nations.

United Nations Economic and Social Council, *Basic Principles on the Use of Restorative Justice Programmes in Criminal Matters*, Resolutions and Decisions Adopted by the Social Council and its Substantive Session of 2002/12, accessed 12 November 2006, http://www.library.dal.ca/law/Guides/RestPathfinder/RestorativeDeclarationpdf.pdf.

Vandeginste, S, 'Victims of genocide, crimes against humanity, and war crimes in Rwanda: the legal and institutional framework of their right to reparation', in J Torpey (ed) *Politics and the Past: On Repairing Historical Injustices*, 2003, Lanham, NJ: Rowman and Littlefeld, pp 249–74.

Van Krieken, R, 'Legal informalism, power and liberal governance', *Social and Legal Studies*, 2001, 10:1, pp 5–22.

Van Ness, D and Heetderks Strong, K, *Restoring Justice*, 1997, Cincinnati, OH: Anderson.

Wacquant, L, 'The penalisation of poverty and the rise of neo-liberalism', *European Journal on Criminal Policy and Research*, 2001, 9:4, pp 401–12.

Walgrave, L, 'From community to domination: in search of social values for restorative justice', in E Weitekamp and HJ Kerner (eds) *Restorative Justice: Theoretical Foundations*, 2002, Cullompton: Willan Publishing, pp 71–89.

Wallimann, I and Dobkowski, MN (eds), *Genocide and the Modern Age: Etiology and Case Studies of Mass Death*, 1987, Syracuse, NY: Syracuse University Press.

Warren, ME and Pearse, H (eds), *Designing Democratic Renewal: The British Columbia Citizens' Assembly*, 2007, Cambridge: University of Cambridge Press.

Weitekamp, E, 'The history of restorative justice', in G Johnstone (ed), *A Restorative Justice Reader: Texts, Sources, Context*, 2003, Cullompton: Willan Publishing, pp 111–24.

Weitekamp, E and Kerner, HJ (eds), *Restorative Justice: Theoretical Foundations*, 2002, Cullompton: Willan Publishing.

Woolford, A, 'The limits of justice: certainty, affirmative repair, and aboriginality', *Journal of Human Rights*, 2004, 3:4, pp 429–44.

Woolford, A, *Between Justice and Certainty: Treaty-Making in British Columbia*, 2005, Vancouver, BC: University of British Columbia Press.

Woolford, A and Ratner, RS, 'Nomadic justice: restorative justice on the margins of law', *Social Justice*, 2003, 30:1, pp 177–94.

Woolford, A and Ratner, RS, 'Selling mediation: the marketing of alternative dispute resolution', *Peace and Conflict Studies Journal*, 2005, 12:1, pp 1–21.

Woolford, A and Ratner, RS, 'Mediation games: justice frames', in S Byrne, J Senehi, D Sandole and I Staroste-Sandole (eds) *Conflict Resolution: Core Concepts, Theories, Approaches and Practices*, 2007, London: Routledge.

Woolford, A and Wolejszo, S, 'Collecting on moral debts: reparations, the Holocaust, and the Porrajmos', *Law and Society Review*, 2006, 40:4, pp 871–901.

Wright, M, *Justice for Victims and Offenders: A Restorative Response to Crime*, 1991, Milton Keynes: Open University Press.

Yazzie, R and Zion, JW, 'Navajo restorative justice: the law of equality and justice', in G Johnstone (ed) *A Restorative Justice Reader: Texts, Sources, Context*, 2003, Cullompton: Willan Publishing, pp 144–51.

Young, J, 'From inclusive to exclusive society: nightmares in the European dream', in V Ruggiero, N South and I Taylor (eds) *The New European Criminology: Crime and Social Order in Europe*, 1999, London: Routledge, pp 64–91.

Young, R, 'Just cops doing "shameful" business? Police-led restorative justice and the lessons of research', in G Johnstone (ed) *A Restorative Justice Reader: Texts, Sources, Context*, 2003, Cullompton: Willan Publishing, pp 398–416.

Zehr, H, *Changing Lenses: A New Focus for Crime and Justice*, 1990, Scottdale, PA: Herald.

Zehr, H, 'Justice paradigm shift? Values and visions in the reform process', *Mediation Quarterly*, Spring 1995, 12:3, pp 207–16.

Zehr, H, 'Fundamental principles of restorative justice', in H Zehr (ed) *The Little Book of Restorative Justice*, 2002, Intercourse, PA: Good Books.

Index